9

D1242804

Citizens of Somewhere Else

Citizens of Somewhere Else

Nathaniel Hawthorne and Henry James

Dan McCall

Cornell University Press

Ithaca and London

Copyright © 1999 by Cornell University

First published 1999 by Cornell University Press

Printed in the United States of America

Library of Congress Cataloging-in-Publication

McCall, Dan.
    Citizens of somewhere else : Nathaniel Hawthorne and Henry James / by Dan McCall.
       p.   cm.
    Includes index.
    ISBN 0-8014-3640-0 (cloth : alk. paper).
    1. James, Henry, 1843–1916—Knowledge—Literature.
    2. Americans—Travel—Great Britain—History—19th century.   3. American fiction—19th century—History and criticism.   4. Hawthorne, Nathaniel, 1804–1864—Kno-wledge—America.   5. National characteristics, American, in literature.   6. James, Henry, 1843–1916—Knowledge—America.
    7. Hawthorne, Nathaniel, 1804–1864—Influence.   8. Influence (Literary, artistic, etc.)   9. United States—In literature. I. Title.
    PS2127.L5M38   1999
    813'.4—dc21   98-36633

Cloth printing   10 9 8 7 6 5 4 3 2 1

In Memory of My Mother
Velma Hooper McCall
1908–1983

Contents

Acknowledgments

For the subject of this book I have chosen two nineteenth-century American writers, Nathaniel Hawthorne and Henry James, about whom hundreds of books have been written. Hasn't everything interesting already been said? Obviously I don't think so; in the following pages I suggest some new ways of reading Hawthorne, reading James, understanding James's extraordinary kinship with Hawthorne and their vexed obsessions with America (perhaps I should put it in quotation marks, "America").

As a Stanford undergraduate I was introduced to Hawthorne and James by the great critic of them both, Yvor Winters. At the University of California, Berkeley, I learned from Larry Ziff and Henry Nash Smith other ways of looking at our two "citizens of somewhere else." In graduate school at Columbia I studied with three devout Jamesians, F. W. Dupee, Quentin Anderson, and Lionel Trilling. All these scholar-critics valued and wrote in a language that a relatively educated layperson could understand. I couldn't have written this book without their inspiring example. I needed, too, the generous help of my colleagues here at Cornell, M. H. Abrams, Glenn Altschuler, Archie Ammons, Jonathan Bishop, Jean Blackall, Elaine Engst, Lamar Herrin, Joel Porte, Edgar Rosenberg, and Michael Steinberg. I am greatly indebted to experts and friends elsewhere: Thomas R. Arp, Richard Brodhead, Michael Colacurcio, Robert Dawidoff,

Stephen Donadio, Barbara Duclos, Daniel Fogel, Betty Friedlander, and Bert O. States.

My greatest debt is to my students, who have made Ithaca a wonderfully lively home for me.

Finally, I have made use of essays of mine, much expanded here, in the following journals: *American Literature, American Quarterly, College English, ELH,* the *Henry James Review,* the *New England Quarterly,* the *New England Review,* and *Nineteenth-Century Literature.* The editors at the Cornell University Press have graciously allowed me to use as my first chapter the foreword they commissioned me to write for their re-issue of James's classic *Hawthorne.*

D. Mc.

Hawthorne in 1848. Courtesy, Peabody Essex Museum, Salem, Mass.

James in 1860. By permission of the Houghton Library,
Harvard University (MS Am1094).

"I am a citizen of somewhere else."
    Nathaniel Hawthorne, "The Custom-House,"
    introductory to *The Scarlet Letter*

Chapter One

Henry James on Nathaniel Hawthorne

Henry James's *Hawthorne* (1879) is an essential text in American cultural history. James wrote the book for the English Men of Letters series; he was the only American contributor, Hawthorne the only American subject. Edmund Wilson was not altogether accurate when he famously claimed in *The Shock of Recognition* (1943) that *Hawthorne* was "the first extended study ever made of an American writer." Before it there had been several "extended studies" of Edgar Allan Poe both in America and France, valuable "appreciations" of Walt Whitman starting as early as the 1860s, and William Gilmore Simms's critical assessments of James Fenimore Cooper. But Wilson was surely right to rank *Hawthorne* as "still one of the best."

Among other achievements James correctly placed *The Scarlet Letter* for us as "the finest piece of imaginative writing yet put forth in the country," and asserted that "something might at last be sent to Europe as exquisite in quality as anything that had been received, and the best of it was that the thing was absolutely American; it belonged to the soil, to the air; it came out of the very heart of New England." But what James so graciously gave with one hand he swiftly took away with the other. In *The Scarlet Letter,* he says, "there is a great deal of symbolism; there is, I think, too much. It is overdone at times, and becomes mechanical; it ceases to be impressive, and grazes triviality. We feel that he goes too far, and is in danger of crossing the line that separates the sublime from its intimate neighbour. We are tempted to say that this is not moral tragedy, but physical comedy." Words to gladden the hearts of all those poor high school students who learned to hate literature and feel dumb by undergoing a forced march through the weird, killjoy prose of this "darksome tale."

When *Hawthorne* was first published, there was considerable public outcry against James's severe tone and general condescension. Who was this traitor to his native land, this expatriate snob who had "gone British" and thumbed his London nose at his predecessor's achievements? James wrote to William Dean Howells that the American critics were "bloodhounds" ferociously drenching "the decent public" with his "gore." In an anonymous review in *The Atlantic* the following month Howells said that "in some quarters" James would be found guilty of "high treason." *Harper's* hoped that the book had been written only in a "momentary fit of indigestion." James called these reviews "a melancholy revelation of angry vanity, vulgarity, and ignorance." He said, "I thought they would protest a good deal at my calling New England life unfurnished, but I didn't expect they would lose their heads and their manners at such a rate." He drew himself up, "prepared to do battle for most of the convictions expressed" in his "little book," but willing to admit some minor faults; he wrote to Howells, "It is quite true I use the word provincial too many times—I hated myself for't, even while I did it (just as I overdo the epithet 'dusky.')" Still, he thought the clamor was "a very big tempest in a very small teapot," and he complained, "What a public to write for!" He hoped "they are not the real American public. If I thought they were, I would give up the country." Who needed such a "clucking of a brood of prairie hens"? For all the bluster we can see he was wounded; this reception really hurt.

Criticism has continued since. F. W. Dupee said of the book, "Its scholarship was weak even for its time (all frankly taken from Lathrop's biography)." James's very first footnote is to that text, *A Study of Hawthorne* (Boston, 1876), written by Hawthorne's son-in-law, George Parsons Lathrop: "Without the help afforded by his elaborate essay the present little volume could not have been prepared." Privately, though, he called Lathrop's work "singularly foolish and pretentious." It is. The Nathaniel Hawthorne who emerges from its pages could not have written the books he did. The son-in-law emphasizes Hawthorne's kindness to his dog Leo, his pity for "some little lambs startled by the approach of his party," and his "fondness for cats," as if his father-in-law's view of the world had been "not that of a fatalist, but of an optimist" with "a very profound faith in Providence" whose "warm, pure, living sympathy pervaded all his analysis of mankind." Lathrop's sentimentality makes him shrink from the "harsh closing chord" of Hawthorne's life—that is, his death—because in "a life so beautiful and noble to surround its ending with the remembrance of mere mortal ailment has in it something of coarseness." It's a garland of wildflowers.

What really got James into trouble with the American custodians of culture was a little list, the most famous passage in the book: "The List" in James's 1879 *Hawthorne:*

> The negative side of the spectacle on which Hawthorne looked out, in his contemplative saunterings and reveries, might, indeed, with a little ingenuity, be made almost ludicrous; one might enumerate the items of high civilisation, as it exists in other countries, which are absent from the texture of American life, until it should become a wonder to know what was left. No State, in the European sense of the word, and indeed barely a specific national name. No sovereign, no court, no personal loyalty, no aristocracy, no church, no clergy, no army, no diplomatic service, no country gentlemen, no palaces, nor manors, nor old country houses, nor parsonages, nor thatched cottages, nor ivied ruins; no cathedrals, nor abbeys, nor little Norman churches; no great Universities nor public schools—no Oxford, nor Eton, nor Harrow; no literature, no novels, no museums, no pictures, no political society, no sporting class—no Epsom nor Ascot! Some such list as that might be drawn up of the absent things in American life.

For half a century critical readers assumed that this laundry list of New England shortcomings and deprivations was a takeoff on a list of Hawthorne's own, in his preface to *The Marble Faun* (the passage is quoted by James just a page before his own); Hawthorne had declared that "no author, without a trial, can conceive of the difficulty of writing a romance about a country where there is no shadow, no antiquity, no mystery, no picturesque and gloomy wrong, not anything but a commonplace prosperity, in broad and simple daylight, as is happily the case with my own dear native land." A curious verdict on America at the very eve of the Civil War. But even so, can this be the real "source" for James's itemized bill? One can hear at least a whisper of it much earlier, in "The New England Holiday" chapter of *The Scarlet Letter,* where Hawthorne lists the absence of "appliances of popular merriment that would have been so readily found in the England of Elizabeth's time": "no rude shows of a theatrical kind; no minstrel with his harp and legendary ballad, nor gleeman with an ape dancing to his music; no juggler with his tricks of mimic witchcraft; no Merry Andrew to stir up the multitude with jests, perhaps hundreds of years old." This sequence goes on to "Wrestling-matches" and other sports such as "an exhibition with the buckler and broadsword," and other peoples, "a party of Indians" and "the crew of the vessel from the Spanish Main"—all those things, in short, that are decidedly *not* of New England and therefore excluded from "the incomplete morality of the age" and its rigid "moral solitude." Here are all the vivid touches and variety of flavors missing from seventeenth-century Boston's claustrophobia.

One can hear later whispers too. For example, in *The Portrait of a Lady* (which James began to write while *Hawthorne* was being debated in America), the cruelly deluded Isabel Archer dresses out Gilbert Osmond's poverties as triumphs: she sees him as a man who has "no property, no title, no honours, no houses, nor lands, nor position, nor reputation, nor brilliant belongings of any sort." All three of these lists go "no . . . no . . . nor. . . nor."

But to know where That Famous List really comes from we are indebted to F. O. Matthiessen and Kenneth Murdock for their monumental edition of James's *Notebooks.* Early on, after one of James's little lists of "*Names*" we find this striking passage (the reader should take special note of the first six words):

In a story some one says—"Oh yes, the United States—a country without a sovereign, without a court, without a nobility, without an army, without a church or a clergy, without a diplomatic service, without a picturesque peasantry, without palaces or castles, or country seats, or ruins, without a literature, without novels, without an Oxford or a Cambridge, without cathedrals or ivied churches, without latticed cottages or village ale-houses, without political society, without sport, without fox-hunting, or country gentlemen, without an Epsom or an Ascot, an Eton or a Rugby!"

Notice that when James puts this list into *Hawthorne* he democratically takes out "a picturesque peasantry" and, aesthetically mindful, he puts in "no museums, no pictures." And adds insult to injury with "no personal loyalty."

The point here is that when we discover that the source of the list is something James wanted someone to say in a story, we realize we are in a brave new context: James speaks as an artist as well as a critic, locating his own powerful energy in both roles, and locating Hawthorne in both roles as well.

Matthiessen says the *Hawthorne* book "is tantalizing in what it omits to say, since it was written at the very period when James was most determined to abandon all traces of romance for realism." James saw Hawthorne as "a man but little disposed to multiply his relations, his points of contact, with society." Hawthorne "was not a man with a literary theory; he was guiltless of a system, and I am not sure that he had ever heard of Realism." And again: "It cannot be too often repeated that Hawthorne was not a realist." In other words, Hawthorne had failed to do exactly what James was now determined to do himself.

Stephen Donadio has powerfully argued that "Hawthorne's own view of his predicament was just the reverse. It was not the paucity of materials that frustrated art, but his own persistent inability to master the abundant (and abundantly complex) materials available to him." We are, that is, bound to recognize that Hawthorne meant it when in "The Custom-House" introductory to *The Scarlet Letter* he gives up on his sketch by saying "a better book than I shall ever write was there" in his experience as a surveyor in Salem, if only he could make sense of all the surrounding details. Lifelong, he makes the same complaint: in *Our Old Home* he wrote that "the Present, the Immediate, the Actual has proved too potent for me. It takes away not only my scanty faculty, but even my desire for imaginative composition." James laments that in *The Scarlet Letter* there is "little elaboration of detail, of the modern realism of research." He concludes that "the faults of the book are, to my sense, a want of reality and an abuse of the fanciful element." Hawthorne's novels do not have what James would later call, in his great phrase, "the solidity of specification" upon which novelistic success "helplessly and submissively depends." James's move to England and the Continent, along with his program of "Realism," is an effort to mark out a place for himself, a way out of what trapped his mentor. Indeed, how could poor old Hawthorne achieve solidity of specification when poor old New England had no solidity to specify? No wonder, then, the angry hubbub in Boston!

But *Hawthorne* was written when Henry James was in his mid-thirties, still a relatively young man, with all his major work ahead of him. For Herman Melville Nathaniel Hawthorne had been an immediate and profoundly enabling presence, as the dedicatory note to *Moby-Dick* so grandly makes clear: "In token of my admiration for his genius, this book is inscribed to Nathaniel Hawthorne." Hawthorne–Melville is a great subject for study; Hawthorne–James is a trickier problem. If you have a mind to, you can see Nathaniel Hawthorne in Henry James's work at the very beginning, in the middle years, and perhaps most impressively in the last masterpieces. Everywhere you look in James, you find Hawthorne.

Lionel Trilling outlines with great elegance what he sees as one of the central flaws in James's 1879 argument: "To the religious elements of Hawthorne's stories, James gives no credence beyond an aesthetic one." Puritanism was just a "pigment." All that James would grant to Hawthorne was that "His imagination 'borrowed' a 'color' and 'reflected' a 'hue.' " Trilling concludes that "James is unequivocal and emphatic in his belief that Hawthorne's interest in Puritanism was nothing but artistic." Trilling wonders, "What are we to do with a judgment of this sort—how are we to escape its embarrassments?"

In several ways. First, Hawthorne at the time James wrote the book was very different from "Our Hawthorne" (Trilling's title) today. Standing roughly midway between James's and ours, interestingly enough, is D. H. Lawrence's "sugary, blue-eyed little darling of a Nathaniel." We sometimes forget that in Hawthorne's own time he was celebrated as the author of *A Wonder-Book for Girls and Boys, Tanglewood Tales,* and other "baby stories," as Hawthorne called them. Richard Brodhead has cautioned us to remember that in the nineteenth century, the *Victorian* era, Hawthorne's "domestic and juvenile pieces were as authentic a part of his oeuvre as the darker tales we value now." Second, the genteel tone of Victorian "high criticism" was one of sweetness and light—"charm" and "sentiment" were key terms, the "pure" and "ethereal" were paramount virtues—and certain orthodox pieties prevailed (Lathrop at least knew his audience). Third, when James says that Hawthorne "contrived to transmute this heavy moral burden into the substance of the imagination" and that "what pleased him in such subjects was their picturesqueness, their rich duskiness of color, their chiaroscuro" we find here an example of what Henry James frequently does when he talks about literary excellence—especially when it deeply moves him—he speaks of writing as if it were painting. The verdicts are hardly sentimental pictures: "It may be said that when his fancy was strongest and keenest, when it was most itself, then the dark Puritan tinge showed in it most richly." And, again, James is young; as he grows older and creates his mature work, his sense of Hawthorne grows up along with him.

In one of the most beautiful sentences of the 1879 book James writes "that the flower of art blooms only where the soil is deep, that it takes a great deal of history to produce a little literature, that it needs a complex social machinery to set a writer in motion." This is the goal of James's passionate pilgrimage—though he is always mindful that "Hawthorne forfeited a precious advantage in ceasing to tread his native soil." Yet James never forsakes Hawthorne; he returns to him almost obsessively, again and again. For example, James complains of *The Blithedale Romance* that "we cease to feel beneath our feet the firm ground of an appeal to our own vision of the world" and that we need a great deal more "about the little community in which its earlier scenes are laid." James makes note "of the absence of satire in the novel, of its not aiming in the least at satire," and there is "no reproduction of strange types of radicalism." Six years later, in *The Bostonians* James attends to each and every one of these defects. Hawthorne's romance and James's novel are both about women's rights, New England, reform movements—and even little details count: in *Blithedale* Westervelt's false teeth are visible in his spooky displays with the Veiled Lady, and in *The Bostonians* we see Selah Tarrant's "terrible smile" when he goes into his creepy routines with his daughter. Very big things count, too: James said of *Blithedale* that "the portion of the story that strikes me as least felicitous is that which deals with Priscilla, and with her mysterious relation to Zenobia." So when the time comes for James to do his own version of the story, he explores, as Millicent Bell remarks, "the bond between Olive and Verena, making it more deeply and exactly penetrative of such a relation than any novel had ever done before." Indeed, it is almost comic the way these two books balance and complement each other: Hollingsworth and Basil Ransom both save the frail, vaguely sappy heroines by marrying them at the last minute, whisking them away from mesmerists. The painful and the tragic also resonate: Olive's vision of the body of a drowned "unknown young woman, defaced beyond recognition, but with long auburn hair and in a white dress" takes us right back to *Blithedale* and Zenobia's watery grave.

Another sort of tribute—another kind of dependency—occurs in one of James's finest novellas, *The Aspern Papers.* Many critics still think of the long-dead poet, Jeffrey Aspern, as Byron or Shelley (both appear in the source anecdote James recorded in his *Notebook*). But when James wrote the story, the English genius turned into an American one, and everything about him we have seen before. He is Hawthorne. One passage is worth quoting at length:

> He had lived in the days before the general transfusion. It had happened to me to regret that he had known Europe at all; I should have liked to see what he would have written without that experience, by which he had incontestably been enriched. But as his fate had ruled otherwise I went with him—I tried to judge how the general old order would have struck him. It was not only there, however, I watched him; the relations he had entertained with the special new had even a livelier interest. His own country after all had had most of his life, and his muse, as they said at that time, was essentially American. That was originally what I had prized him for: that at a period when our native land was nude and crude and provincial, when the famous "atmosphere" it is supposed to lack was not even missed, when literature was lonely there and art and form almost impossible, he had found means to live and write like one of the first; to be free and general and not at all afraid; to feel, understand and express everything.

Change each and every "he" to "Hawthorne," and it works perfectly. There's the little play on The List, a clever nod to the consulship at Liverpool and the residence in Rome, and, of course, the entire conception: "one of the first," the "essentially American." Who speaks here?—our slippery unnamed narrator or Henry James himself, who had said exactly the same things about Hawthorne a decade earlier?

Back in 1872, in a review of Hawthorne's *French and Italian Notebooks,* James called Hawthorne "the last pure American." Seven years later, discussing Hawthorne's European sojourn, James wrote, "I know nothing more remarkable, more touching, than the sight of this odd, youthful-elderly mind, contending so late in the day with new opportunities for learning old things, and, on the whole, profiting by them so freely and gracefully." And whom have we here? In an astonishing prevision—the hero of *The Ambassadors,* Lambert Strether to perfection!

And in a formal literary sense, James's prefaces to the great New York edition of his work, the most stunningly brilliant exercise in practical criticism ever written, are indebted to the Hawthorne whom James cited as "in general never more graceful than when prefatory." One can see Hawthorne's compulsive distinctions in his prefaces between Romance and Novel—especially the one to *The House of The Seven Gables*—in James's sly preface to *The American:* "There have been, I gather, many definitions of romance, as a matter indispensably of boats, or of caravans, or of tigers, or of 'historical characters,' or of ghosts, or of forgers, or of detectives, or of beautiful wicked women, or of pistols and knives." This too is Hawthornean in its lovely humor, conversational ease, and laconic discriminations.

In 1896 James wrote another critical and biographical essay on Hawthorne for Charles Dudley Warner's *Library of the World's Best Literature.* James's article is more sophisticated and frankly passionate than his *Hawthorne* of seventeen years earlier. James now sees that his predecessor's "great complication was the pressing moral anxiety, the restless individual conscience . . . the laws secretly broken, the impulses secretly felt, the hidden passions, the double lives, the dark corners, the closed rooms, the skeletons in the cupboard and at the feast." A "list" again, but what a difference—the morally picturesque has become the darker psychology. This is a profounder Hawthorne than James had known before (and never before known so intimately). It is the Hawthorne who was "happy in an appetite that could find a feast in meagre materials." And in "The Beast in the Jungle," for example, the very *idea* of the story, with no stretching at all, can be located in Hawthorne's own notebook: "Two persons to be expecting some occurrence, and watching for the two principal actors in it, and to find that the occurrence is even then passing, and that they themselves are the two actors." Once again, Richard Brodhead has the matter exactly right: "It is, uncannily, as if Hawthorne had become the real author." Like crazy Wakefield and that suffering Minister who put on the black veil, John Marcher is possessed—from out of nowhere, at least from out of nowhere he knows—by a hideous curse which fatally separates man from woman and all "domestic affections." James had begun this story by asking, "What is there in the idea of *Too Late?*" As Matthiessen and Murdock point out, James was now doing his work in the Hawthorne way: "he started with an abstraction and sought an embodiment for it." And the story proceeds as Hawthorne's best usually do; it is what James called "a negative adventure." Hawthorne was now on James's mind more deeply than any other writer he had ever read.

Nearing the end of his long, great life, James bids a final goodbye to Hawthorne. In *Notes of a Son and Brother* he writes that Hawthorne's work "was all charged with a *tone,* a full and rare tone" which was "for me, at least—ever so appreciably American; which proved to what a use American matter could be put by an American hand" and proved also that "an American could be an artist, one of the finest, without 'going outside' about it . . . quite in fact as if Hawthorne had become one just by being American *enough.*" Had he not said as much almost forty years ago? Suddenly, the instinctive grasp of a young artist concludes in the radiant apprehension of an aging master. Once again, as James says, "Hawthorne is the most valuable example of the American genius."

Chapter Two

Adaptations and Borrowings

Upon first reading Nathaniel Hawthorne, my Cornell students usually like least about him what I love most—his prose style. For them his archaic manner is too heavy-going (all that symbolism!); it's stuffy, boring, ancient history. For me the style is powerful, supple, thoroughly original—an invention so utterly his own that you can no more mistake a Hawthorne paragraph for somebody else's than you can misattribute a Van Gogh painting.

To coax the class out of their Castle Dismal, I show them what a rich source Hawthorne was for two poets, Robert Lowell and Emily Dickinson. Lowell's poem is from something Hawthorne wrote very late in life, and Dickinson's takes off from a dark sketch Hawthorne wrote very early, probably in college.

Returning to America after his years of consulship in Liverpool and his anxious, terrible months in Italy (his daughter Una had almost died of "Roman fever"), Hawthorne worked on four different "Romances." He was unable to complete any one of them. He still has power, terrific power, in these abortive adventures, but in each book he flirts with a subject, stops momentarily to throw intense light on a problem, and then wanders away in search of bloody footprints and magic potions. Nowhere does he seem to see the real significance of his symbols, what they represented for him about his own aging as a writer and as a man. But we should listen to the exquisite music of those fragments:

> No; the proud and vivid and active prospects that had heretofore spread themselves before him—the striving to conquer, the struggle, the victory, the defeat, if such it was to be,—the experience for good or ill,— the life, life, life—all possibility of these was passing from him; all that hearty earnest contest or communion of man with man; and leaving him nothing but this great sombre shade, this brooding of the old family mansion . . . the mansion itself was like dark-colored experience, the reality; the point of view where things were seen in their true lights; the true world, all outside of which was delusion, and here— dreamlike as its structures seemed—the absolute truth.
>
> "Dr. Grimshawe's Secret"

> In short, it was such a moment as I suppose all men feel (at least, I can answer for one), when the real scene and picture of life swims, jars, shakes, seems about to be broken up and dispersed, like the picture in a smooth pond, when we disturb its tranquil mirror by throwing in a stone; and though the scene soon settles itself, and looks as real as before, a haunting doubt keeps close at hand, as long as we live, asking, "Is it stable? Am I sure of it? Am I certainly not dreaming?" See; it trembles again, ready to dissolve.
>
> "Septimius Felton"

> He muttered, sitting by himself, long, indistinct masses of talk, in which this name was discernible, and other names. Going on mumbling, by the hour together, great masses of vague trouble, in which, if only it could have been unravelled and put in order, no doubt all the secrets of his life might have been found. His mind evidently wandered.
>
> "Dr. Grimshawe's Secret"

> Walking the streets seldom and reluctantly, he felt a dreary impulse to elude the people's observation, as if with a sense that he had gone irrevocably out of fashion, and broken his connecting links with the net-work of human life; or else it was that nightmare feeling which we

sometimes have in dreams, when we seem to find ourselves wandering through a crowded avenue, with the noonday sun upon us, in some wild extravagance of dress or nudity. He was conscious of estrangement from his towns-people, but did not always know how nor wherefore, nor why he should be thus groping through the twilight mist in solitude.

"The Dolliver Romance"

The pain in these paragraphs is overwhelming, and the prose is as beautiful as any Hawthorne ever wrote. These fine passages are, finally, preparations for an epitaph.

One of them serves that function through its rediscovery and conversion into poetic lines, Robert Lowell's "Hawthorne," first published at the front of the Ohio State *Hawthorne Centenary Essays* in 1964. Lowell's verse draws on Hawthorne's prose; the line "along a flat, unvaried surface," for example, is straight out of "The Custom-House." But perhaps only an academic specialist could be expected to hear the most elaborate echo in the poem, for few readers have pondered at length over the fragmentary romance "Septimius Felton." The last eleven lines of Lowell's poem are taken almost verbatim from a sentence in Hawthorne's draft of this book he never finished. Near the beginning of the story, Hawthorne describes his title figure:

As for Septimius, let him alone for a moment or two, and then they would see him, with his head bent down, brooding, brooding, his eyes fixed on some chip, some stone, some common plant, any commonest thing, as if it were the clew and index to some mystery; and when, by chance startled out of these meditations, he lifted his eyes, there would be a kind of perplexity, a dissatisfied, foiled look in them, as if of his speculations he found no end.

In his poem Lowell tightens the sentence, slightly; he emphasizes the subtle local effects in the prose ("and you'll see him with his head / bent down") and substitutes for "startled out of these meditations" the more deliberate slow rising of the eyes. But mainly Lowell lets Hawthorne speak for himself:

Leave him alone for a moment or two,
And you'll see him with his head
bent down, brooding, brooding
eyes fixed on some chip,
some stone, some common plant,
the commonest thing,
as if it were the clew.
The disturbed eyes rise,
furtive, foiled, dissatisfied
from meditation on the true
and insignificant.

Coming as the sentence does, at the end of Lowell's poem, it reverberates full force. In Hawthorne the effect is largely wasted in a lengthy paragraph about "these young people, on that beautiful spring morning, sitting on the hill-side." The sentence follows a thoroughly conventional portrait of Robert Hagburn, a "ruddy, burly young fellow, handsome and free of manner, six feet high, famous through the neighborhood for strength and athletic skill" (a man in the long line of Hawthorne's "blacksmiths" who thwart his "artists of the beautiful"), and in turn is followed by Robert and Rose Garfield "running on with gay talk." In the original the sentence is doomed to blush unseen, as were all of these late, masterful fragments, lost in a tangle of pointless details.

In a little preface to *Septimius Felton,* published posthumously in 1871, Una Hawthorne wrote that she felt the book deserved to be printed in its unfinished form because it was "a striking specimen of the peculiarities and charms of his style, and that it will have an added interest for brother artists." For Lowell the "peculiarities and charm" of Hawthorne's style obviously proved compelling, and in his creative modulations of that style he has given it the "added interest" of a tragic portrait of Hawthorne himself.

But why would Robert Lowell be reading *Septimius Felton*? I strongly suspect he wasn't. Lowell had written a brilliant essay, "Yvor Winters" (1961); in Winters's definitive chapter on Hawthorne in *In Defense of Rea-*

son he quotes the very same passage from "Septimius Felton." Winters cites the critic Percy Boynton, who had already quoted the passage and referred to it as "a self-portrait" of Hawthorne.

When we face a problem of indebtedness, any example of the "anxiety of influence," we must make sure we can answer the question of where *exactly* something comes from. It makes perfect sense to see Lowell turning to Winters on Hawthorne rather than to an obscure passage in Hawthorne's late failures.

In his 1879 *Hawthorne* Henry James said that his subject's "style was excellent from the beginning; he appeared to have passed through no phase of learning how to write, but was in possession of his means, from the first, of his handling a pen." That is true: there are no characteristic "periods" or evolutionary phases in Hawthorne as there are in James. From the beginning we see Hawthorne full-grown. His very brief story "The Hollow of the Three Hills" first appeared in the Salem *Gazette* on November 12, 1830, when Hawthorne was twenty-six; it is one of only two of his earliest stories he included in the *Twice-Told Tales* of 1837. (Edgar Allan Poe gave the story special praise in his review in *Graham's Magazine*.) Very brief indeed, "The Hollow of the Three Hills" seems more like a prose poem, a terrifying vision of guilt and dread, than a story. In "strange old times" a "lady" lays her forehead on the knees of an "aged crone"; cloaked "in darkness" by the robes of the old woman, the lady hears "the muttered words of prayer" and then hushes herself "still as death." In a wilderness of "strange murmurings increasing" and "shrieks" and "singing" and "groaning and sobs, a ghastly confusion of terror and mourning and mirth," three central sounds come out to locate the lady's burdens of guilt as "the daughter who had wrung the aged hearts of her parents,—the wife who had betrayed the trusting fondness of her husband,—the mother who had sinned against natural affection, and left her child to die." The accumulation of guilt, fear, and riotous sound is overpowering; then the voices fade away "like a thin vapor," and "when the old woman stirred the kneeling lady, she lifted not her head." She has been frightened to death. We cannot be sure if the guilt is real or imag-

ined, if the delinquencies are actual events in her past or if they are anxious projections, the "fantastic dreams and madmen's reveries" Hawthorne speaks of in his opening lines.

It takes only ten minutes to read the story aloud, and I do so for my students. Then I write on the blackboard

    - / - / - / - /
    - / - / - /
    - / - / - / - /
    - / - / - /

and explain it so that the students will be able to put together properly
the five stanzas of Emily Dickinson's poem "I Felt a Funeral in my
Brain" (written about 1861 and first published in 1896). I ask the students
to think about "The Hollow of the Three Hills" as I dictate the poem:

I felt a Funeral, in my Brain,
And Mourners to and fro
Kept treading—treading—till it seemed
That sense was breaking through—

And when they all were seated,
A Service, like a Drum—
Kept beating—beating—till I thought
My Mind was going numb—

And then I heard them lift a Box
And creak across my Soul
With those same Boots of Lead, again
Then Space—began to toll,

As all the Heavens were a Bell,
And Being but an Ear,
And I, and silence, some strange Race
Wrecked, solitary, here—

And then a Plank in Reason, broke,
And I dropped down, and down—
And hit a World, at every plunge,
And Finished knowing—then—

The ambiguity of the final line persists in Miss Dickinson's alternative choice of "Got Through" for "Finished." The class and I look at the word "And," the way it begins the second line of the first stanza, the first line of the second stanza, begins lines twice in the third and fourth, and then begins all four lines of the final stanza. We talk a little about the punctuation in her verse (are those really dashes?) and the Germanic–Puritan–Transcendental capital letters. Usually I mention that the poem has been beautifully set to music by Aaron Copland. Then I tell the class about Dickinson's tribute, as only she would put it, "Hawthorne appalls, entices—."

What I most want them to see is that the stage for the action, in both poem and story, is the mind of a lady; Dickinson feels the funeral in her "brain," and the "three hills" in the Hawthorne story are exterior symbols of the lady's inner feelings of guilt as daughter, wife, and mother. In both poem and story the central character is driven to loss of consciousness—and, in both, apparently, to loss of life—by a series of crushing sounds. In the poem there is the suggestion of a pagan rite (and violent headache) in the "Service, like a Drum." In the story, the old hag behaves like a false Priest who hears the confession of the sinner, leads her on, pours forth "the monotonous words of a prayer that was not meant to be acceptable in heaven." The drone cannot offer absolution; at the end she can only chuckle to herself about the "sweet hour's sport!" And the speaker in the poem cannot drop safely, six feet into the earth; instead, she plummets "down, and down—And hit a World, at every plunge." In both story and poem, the death agony is utter, a dreadful outburst expressing, in Hawthorne's words, "a sense of intolerable humiliation."

What is close to uncanny here is that not only do Hawthorne's "lady" and the speaker in Dickinson's poem hear terrible sounds, they hear the same terrible sounds. In "The Hollow of the Three Hills," the lady catches the voice of a man who "went to and fro continually, and his feet sounded upon the floor." In the final paragraph: "Then came a measured tread, passing slowly, slowly on, as of mourners with a coffin." The "mourners" and the "tread" and the "coffin" ("box") all reappear in Dickinson's poem. Hawthorne's lady hears "the knolling of a bell," "a death bell," just as the speaker in the poem hears that "Space—began to toll / As all the Heavens were a Bell." Dickinson's horrifying image of "Being, but an Ear" has its root in Hawthorne's phrases: "voices strengthen upon the ear," and "all these noises deepened and became substantial to the listener's ear," and "the ear could measure the length of their melancholy array" ("ear" in the singular, all three times). And Dickinson's "strange Race" of a "Wrecked" and "solitary" pair can be traced back into "The Hollow of the Three Hills" where the solitary pair of women is stranded in the "deep shades" that threaten "to overspread the world."

The correspondences are several and deep; both works are remarkable chapters in the story of what Hawthorne called "the anxiety that had long been kindling" in the New England mind.

There is something else, something rather important, about "The Hollow of the Three Hills." In *Hawthorne* James compares *The Scarlet Letter* (1850) to the English novel *Adam Blair* (1822) by John Gibson Lockhart: "Each man wrote as his turn of mind impelled him; but each expressed something more than himself. Lockhart was a dense, substantial Briton, with a taste for the concrete, and Hawthorne was a thin New Englander, with a miasmatic conscience." And when we read *Adam Blair* with an attentive eye (and ear!), keeping clearly in mind "The Hollow of the Three Hills," we find an extraordinary kinship. James saw better than he knew. In the very first chapter of *Adam Blair* (this book came out when Hawthorne was a sophomore at Bowdoin) we find that Adam Blair's "footsteps had been heard for some time hurriedly traversing and re-traversing the floor." Blair runs out and throws himself down in the midst of a grove of pines where "the wind moaned and sighed through the darkness about him," and agonizing scenes come to mind—"The mother, that had nursed his years of infancy—the father whose hairs he had long before laid in the grave." Blair starts up and gazes around, and sees "nothing but the sepulchral gloom of the wood and hearing nothing but the cold blasts among the leaves." Later, "an old Highlander crone" discovers him, and "suddenly there came wafted from afar-off the echo of a bell tolling slowly." In chapter 14 Blair rushes out into the forest again, to a pool, "a melancholy tarn, formed where three hills descend into the bosom of the earth together." He sits, and "the anguish of his remorse clothed itself in tangible forms, and his spirit shrunk amidst them, as if he had been surrounded with the presence of real demons"; he sees figures and hears the voice of "scornful curses muttered everywhere round about him." And he kneels.

In one of Hawthorne's greatest stories, "Young Goodman Brown," we are told that at the witches' sabbath on that wild night, "a confused and doubtful sound of voices" was "so indistinct" that Brown "doubted whether he had heard aught but the murmur of the forest." "Sometimes the wind tolled like a distant church bell." "A basin was hollowed, naturally, in the rock." Brown saw "the shape of his own dead father beckoning him to advance," and "Was it his mother?" A woman "threw out her hand to warn him back." The sudden appearance of his wife's pink ribbon made clear to him that he had dishonored and lost her. Taking care of the dead baby, the Devil himself was "the sole guest to an infant's funeral."

Clearly, Hawthorne is paying attention to Lockhart—and, remarkably, continues to pay attention to him for twenty years more. At the end of chapter 2 of *The Scarlet Letter*, when Hester is enduring her "leaden infliction" on the pillory, she sees "in memory's picture-gallery" her native village, "her father's face with its bald brow and reverend white beard, that flowed over the old-fashioned Elizabethan ruff; her mother's, too, with the look of heedful and anxious love" and "another countenance," that of her wronged husband, and then "she clutched the child so fiercely to her breast that it sent forth a cry." Back at the "Hollow," the parents had been "these two old people, the man calmly despondent, the woman querulous and tearful . . . and they spoke of a daughter, a wanderer they knew not where, bearing dishonor along with her, and leaving shame and affliction to bring their gray heads to the grave." The wronged husband "went to and fro continually, and his feet sounded upon the floor," as he "sought an auditor for the story of woman's perfidy, of a wife who had broken her holiest vows, of a home and heart made desolate." Finally, the mother had "left her child to die."

And—one more time—at the end of chapter 11 of *The Scarlet Letter*, Dimmesdale tortures his own face in the looking-glass. Visions flit before

Chapter Three

Hawthorne's "Familiar Kind of Preface"

While Hawthorne's prefaces have been widely remarked upon and anthologized, they are too often taken simply as elaborate definitions of a genre specializing in mellowed light. Their real subject is not aesthetic theory; rather, it is Hawthorne's attempt to borrow a commonplace of literary theory in the mid-nineteenth century, the distinction between Romance and Novel, in order to mitigate his sense of failing his materials and the best in his own talent. We must maintain a double awareness of the fight going on in him and in his writing between what Poe called "the obvious" and "the insinuated." If we do not hear the man's voice while he makes his definitions, if we do not realize what went into the prefaces, then we cannot claim to understand what they are and why Hawthorne was compelled to write them.

He was never quite sure what to think about his own work. In "Fragments From The Journal Of A Solitary Man" he confessed, in the person of his tubercular young artist, that "I have never yet discovered the real secret of my powers." And in spite of his many prefatory essays on what he was trying to do, Hawthorne failed to make a statement that satisfied him; he lived in uneasy contradictions. His son, Julian, once said: "My father was two men." Hawthorne does often present himself as two men, intently scrutinizing each other, each daring the other to cross the line. His "Inmost Me" and his "iron reserve" engage in constant disruptive combat. The conflict was not only in his writing itself—the tension registered as a war between an eighteenth-century style and a nineteenth-century romantic, symbolist's way of seeing the world—but also between the writer and the man. When, after his father's death, Julian got around to reading the novels, he was "unable to comprehend how a man such as I knew my father to be could have written such books. He did not talk in that way, his moods had not seemed to be of that color." And Julian concludes that "the man and the writer were, in Hawthorne's case, as different as a mountain from a cloud." In writing the novels, half of Hawthorne's mind told him that in mellowing the lights and enriching the shadows he was concentrating on essentials; he said to himself that what he lacked in realistic portraiture of details he gained by freeing himself to contemplate the "deeper import" of his subject. But to that idea another part of him said no, and his sympathies remained divided.

As the editor of *The American Magazine of Useful and Entertaining Knowledge* he wrote that his job was to "Concoct, concoct." The phrase could be used—as James's warning to himself, "Dramatize, Dramatize!" has been used to describe his method—to sum up how Hawthorne worked. He advised himself "Make all dreamlike." And where he succeeded he was able to convey the resonant imagery of dreams, their displacements and symbolic admissions; where he failed he made his work not "dreamlike " but only dreamy, a vague wash of fluttering shapes. Turning his back on the accurate and copious notebooks, he wrote to Longfellow that he was plagued by "lack of materials." He complained that he had "nothing but thin air to concoct my stories of, and it is not easy to give a life-like semblance to such shadowy stuff." The complaint is curious since, when he wanted to, he could render marvelously little facts around him and the high points of colonial history. In his prefaces, however, he sets off actuality and allegorical significance as if a choice were involved between the representation of a thing and the meaning of a thing. Hawthorne often presents his job as a choice between detail and moral. His notebooks betray a mind operating at two extremes: either "An abstraction to be symbolized" or, jotting down a realistically treated incident, "What can I make of it?" He starts from either end, and then tries to work it out: to find embodiment for his abstraction or meaning for his symbol.

Often unable to find either of them around him, he wrote in several prefaces that art should inhabit "cloud land." Yet he never quite convinced himself that cloud land was a good place to write from, and in all his definitions of " psychological romance " there is the sense of regret, the sense of something missed. In the person of Aubépine (in the headnote to "Rappaccini's Daughter") he found himself "too remote, too shadowy, and unsubstantial in his modes of development" so that his "inveterate love of allegory" invested "his plots and characters with the aspect of scenery and people in the clouds," and stole away "the human warmth out of his conceptions." Throughout his commentary on his writing Hawthorne keeps telling us how his stories are "ethereal" and then complaining that they are "cold."

Perhaps a central reason for his choosing to inhabit those "cloud lands" was that they provided a cover for "the Real Me." In "The Old Manse" he wrote that "so far as I am a man of really individual attributes I veil my face; nor am I, nor have I ever been, one of those supremely hospitable people who serve up their own hearts, delicately fried, with brain sauce, as a tidbit for their beloved public." In his preface to *The Snow Image* he begins by saying that some find him "egotistical, indiscreet, and even impertinent on account of the Prefaces and Introductions," but then goes on to say that they "hide the man, instead of displaying him." In a letter to her mother, in October 1842, Sophia Hawthorne wrote of her husband that "his vocation is to observe and not to be observed." His friend, Horatio Bridge, said of him that "he shrank habitually from the exhibition of his own secret opinions." And D. H. Lawrence made the classic formula: "our blue-eyed darling Nathaniel knew disagreeable things in his inner soul. He was careful to send out his secrets in disguise."

It is important to remember that when Hawthorne made his definitions of Romance he was drawing on a commonplace. In England Sir Walter Scott and Edward Bulwer-Lytton elaborated the characteristics of The Romance, distinguishing it from the novel; Scott described Romance as a "fictitious narrative in prose or verse, the interest of which turns upon marvellous and uncommon incidents." For Scott the novel was different from the Romance because the events in a novel were common, not marvelous, and they were portrayed in the context of modern society. In America, William Gilmore Simms said in his preface to *The*

Yemassee (1835), "You will note that I call *The Yemassee* a romance, and not a novel. You will permit me to insist on the distinction." And James Fenimore Cooper, in his preface to the final collection of the Leatherstocking tales, wrote that his work "aspired to the elevation of Romance"; he conceived of that genre as somehow better and truer than the novel. Hawthorne often gave voice to much the same idea, but he could not go along the whole way and often turns to an irony that takes back the definition in the very act of making it. In the introductory note to *The Blithedale Romance* he complains that America lacks the necessary atmosphere for Romance; the "beings" of the author's imagination

> are compelled to show themselves in the same category as actually living mortals; a necessity that generally renders the paint and paste-board of their composition but too painfully discernible. With the idea of partially obviating this difficulty (the sense of which has always pressed very heavily upon him), the author has ventured to make free with his old and affectionately remembered home at BROOK FARM as being certainly the most romantic episode of his own life, essentially a day-dream, and yet a fact, and thus offering an available foothold between fiction and reality.

How serious is this passage? Brook Farm was not altogether "affectionately remembered"—not in his notes, letters, or lawsuit. His early enthusiasm for the project died within a few months; when he wrote the above note on the experiment almost ten years had passed, a decade in which his pessimism about visionary schemes had deepened. How serious, in all Hawthorne's prefaces, are the continuing complaints that the shades are too retired and that he was only trying to write "a fanciful story, evolving a thoughtful moral?" In the repeated objections and disclaimers he seems at times a bit too satisfied with his limitations. To be sure, there is a good deal of the self-conscious and amused dismay of an artist trying to speak about his own work. But in the light of Hawthorne's difficulties and choices one can see much more: often the irony in the prefatory remarks is self-indulgent rather than self-critical, a public pose.

He felt that art should " spiritualize reality." In the forest scene of *The Scarlet Letter* Pearl sees herself in one of the pools formed by the little brook. The pool "reflected a perfect image of her little figure; with all the brilliant picturesqueness of her beauty in its adornment of flowers and wreathed foliage, but more defined and spiritualized than the reality." It is not unfair to Hawthorne's aesthetic to say that throughout his life he tended to think that the function of his art was to work like the little pool. In the person of the pilgrim to "The Hall of Fantasy" (1843), Hawthorne concludes his visit by insisting that he is not content to have the world "exist merely in idea"; he wants "her great round, solid self to endure interminably." But, he quickly adds, "nevertheless" he "almost desired that the whole of life might be spent in that visionary scene where the actual world with its hard angles should never rub against me and only be viewed through the medium of picture windows." His final observation is that the Hall is good "for the sake of spiritualizing the grossness of this actual life."

So, Hawthorne's aim as an artist is based, first of all, on an ideal of refinement, refinement that seeks a purity in which physical and material things literally fade out of the picture. Yet Hawthorne is oddly reluctant to stand by that ideal and continually goes back on it in irony, saying (to quote the most famous example) that if you open a book of his in strong sunlight it will appear to be only blank pages. When he assesses his work as "the faintest possible counterfeit of real life," the question I am trying to answer is: why did he fail to manufacture a more direct and detailed counterfeit? He did not wish his work to be judged by the laws of everyday probability. In his faltering notes for *The Ancestral Footstep* he wrote that he did "not wish it to be a picture of real life, but a Romance. . . . In the introduction I might disclaim all intention to draw a real picture." That theme, late in his life, appears early and continuously in his writing; throughout his sketch "Main Street" the quarrel between the showman and the critic is: How should the world be seen? "The critic," constantly concerned with "things just the way they are," does not tolerate the art of the Romancer. The showman keeps telling the critic to move farther away, to take another point of view. "I ask pardon of the audience," he says.

But if we look closely, we can see that in the sketch Hawthorne is not just asking pardon of a hostile public; in one sense, the two halves of Hawthorne are talking to each other. Throughout his writing he is a man answering himself. To read his prefaces properly, one must be alive to his indecision; there was warfare between his intuition that his books were botched and his attempts to turn their deficiencies into virtues. Although his relation to his art and his relation to his audience are necessarily interdependent, I will separate them to explore his ideas about the works themselves and then to examine his hopes and fears about the people who would read them.

Any "American" work, something produced on this side of the Atlantic and not pirated from England, could expect favorable reviews, at least from *The Literary World* or *Graham's Magazine*. The only real complaint from these quarters when *The Scarlet Letter* appeared was that the book did not properly balance its emotions and tones. "Mixture of feeling," "laughter and tears," "sunshine" and "shadows"—these combinations were the ideal formulas (stemming from the admiration in America for Dickens's novels and Shakespeare's plays). What the reviewers wanted was both humor and pathos weaving around each other in the story. But in *The Scarlet Letter* Hawthorne had not sufficiently adulterated his adultery; the classic objection is Edwin Percy Whipple's review of *Gables* in *Graham's Magazine* for June 1851, where he says that "the error in *The Scarlet Letter* proceeded from the divorce of its humor from its pathos—the introduction being as genial as Goldsmith or Lamb, and the story which followed being tragic even to ghastliness. In the *House of Seven Gables* the humor and the pathos are combined." Thus, not only Hawthorne himself but also his reviewers said that *Gables* was better than *The Scarlet Letter*: laughter and tears evened out (and, after all, the subject of an old family mansion was a good deal easier on New England nerves than *The Scarlet Letter*).

Yet when Hawthorne consciously tried to give his deepest insights comic relief he squandered the emotional energy of his story. The "humor and pathos" in *Gables* fail to combine with real force. One must turn Whipple on his head: the great virtue of "The Custom-House" is that it takes the mixed genre quite out of *The Scarlet Letter* itself so that the story of seventeenth-century Boston stays pure and formally coherent. One could go so far as to say, a trifle crudely but not inaccurately, that "The Custom-House" *is* "Novel," in Hawthorne's mind, and *The Scarlet Letter is* "Romance." The following year Hawthorne makes the clarification in the preface to *Gables:* a Novel "is presumed to aim at a very minute fidelity, not merely to the possible, but to the probable and ordinary course of man's experience." To apply novelistic standards "exposes the Romance to an inflexible and exceedingly dangerous species of criticism, by bringing fancy-pictures almost into positive contact with the realities of the moment," and that "it has been no part of his object to describe local manners." The book should be read as "a legend prolonging itself," and the dark, gabled house is built "of materials long in use for constructing castles in the air."

There is a funny contradiction here. The "moonshiny" romance needs to be protected from the harsh sunlight of "the actual." But the romance in its devious darkness generates more power. In "The Devil in Manuscript" the man responsible for setting the town on fire is a writer; he throws all his romances into the roaring fireplace; the sparks go up the chimney and hop from thatched roof to roof in municipal conflagration. The title of the story is a statement of Hawthorne's attitude: "The Devil in Manuscript" (he was quite literally there, or, as Hawthorne elsewhere complains, in the inkwell). The fire in the story is as demonic as the laugh that concludes it. For Hawthorne, art was associated with insidious force. In "The Art of Fiction" James writes on this subject that

"Art" in our Protestant communities, where so many things have got so strangely twisted about, is supposed in certain circles to have some vague injurious effect upon those who make it an important consideration, who let it weigh in the balance. It is assumed to be opposed in some mysterious manner to morality, to amusement, to instruction. When it is embodied in the work of a painter (the sculptor is another affair!) you know what it is; it stands there before you, in the honesty of pink and green and a gilt frame; you can see the worst of it at a glance, and you can be on your guard. But when it is introduced into literature it becomes more insidious—there is danger of its hurting you before you know it.

James can show off splendidly when he wishes to, and he wishes to here; the indictment he makes of the community is a successfully balanced expression of his half-amused and half-outraged distaste for the American idea of art. But James's indictment, so civilized, should not obscure his great terror about "the vague injurious effect" art had "upon those who make it an important consideration, who let it weigh in the balance" and the price great art would cost him. Hawthorne lies somewhere between James and the stuffy community that James attacks. Hawthorne's deep misgivings about art were similar to James's: writing involved a "certain chilliness, a want of earnestness," which made the writer less than a man, unable to respond with any liveliness or spontaneity to experience, never living, always taking notes. Miles Coverdale and John Marcher are projections of their authors, each character an image of what the man most feared about himself and his craft. But Hawthorne's frequent retreats into piousness reflect his unsuccessful resistance to the community's assumptions that art is "opposed in some mysterious manner to morality, to amusement, to instruction." He meant it when he wrote to Fields, "I wish God had given me the faculty of writing a sunshiny book." In remarking that "my own individual taste is for quite another class of works than those which I myself am able to write," he was telling the truth.

We may perhaps define now, with greater precision, why Hawthorne was such a determined frequenter of "cloud land." Northrop Frye has written in *The Anatomy of Criticism* of the distinction between Novel and Romance; Frye's account is perhaps closer to explaining Hawthorne's predicament than anything Hawthorne himself said in his prefaces:

> The essential difference between novel and romance lies in the conception of characterization. The romancer does not attempt to create "real people" so much as stylized figures which expand into psychological archetypes. It is in the romance that we find Jung's libido, anima, and shadow reflected in the hero, heroine, and villain respectively. That is why the romance so often radiates a flow of subjective intensity that the novel lacks, and why a suggestion of allegory is constantly creeping in around its fringes.

Hawthorne was working in this realm of "subjective intensity" imperfectly contained and defined by the "suggestion of allegory" on its fringes, a world that sparked with something untamable. It was a world that violated his theory of art as prim refinement. He wrote to Sophia that we are shadows until the heart is touched: "that touch creates us—then we begin to be." But he could not tolerate much more than that one touch. There is an intimate connection between his aesthetic ideal of how art should "spiritualize" life and his responses to women. In *Fanshawe* he writes of his heroine, Ellen, that illness produced "not a disadvantageous change in her appearance" for she "was paler and thinner; her countenance was more intellectual, more spiritual." Slightness of figure, even this faint hint of illness, was Hawthorne's idea of feminine beauty, and as we have seen, it was also his idea of the art of "Romance," something withdrawn from life and "more intellectual, more spiritual." The description of Priscilla's face in the fourth chapter of *Blithedale* is couched in exactly the same terms as Hawthorne's famous description of his tales: "a wan, almost sickly hue, betokening habitual seclusion from the sun and free of atmosphere, like a flower-shrub that had done its best to blossom in too scanty light." One of the mysterious moralisms in *Septimius Felton* reads: "Kiss no woman if her lips be red; look not upon her if she be very fair."

Hawthorne shows us his response to a woman who was "very fair," a woman he observed at a Lord Mayor's reception dinner in England. He writes in his notebooks that his "eyes were most drawn to a young lady who sat nearly opposite me, across the table." He then devotes a full page to her beauty: "Her hair . . . a wonderful deep, raven black, black as night, black as death; *not* raven black, for that has a shiny gloss, and hers had not; but it was hair never to be painted, nor described—wonderful hair . . . all her features were so fine that sculpture seemed a despicable art beside her." And while she makes him fly for comparisons to Rachel and Judith and Bathsheba and Eve, he concludes: "I never should have thought of touching her, nor desired to touch her; for, whether owing to distinctness of race, my sense that she was a Jewess, or whatever else, I felt a sort of repugnance, simultaneously with my perception that she was an admirable creature."

The retreat to "cloud land" becomes clearer. Hawthorne's intense evasiveness, perhaps most clearly demonstrated in this passage from his notebooks, enters and controls some of the most complex relationships in his fiction, usually in somewhat the same form we find it here, a reserved and literary man responding to a richly luxuriant woman, as in Coverdale to Zenobia, Dimmesdale to Hester, Giovanni to Rappaccini's Daughter. And while Hawthorne renders these relationships with extraordinary intensity, he also seems unable to gain a complete grasp of his images and events. Sophia wrote to Chorley that "Mr. Hawthorne is driven by his muse, but he does not drive her; and I have known him to be in an inextricable doubt, in the midst of a book or sketch, as to its probable issue." So much in doubt that when Sophia asked him if Beatrice Rappaccini was to be a demon or angel, Hawthorne replied, according to Julian, "I have no idea." When he gave the original manuscript of *The Scarlet Letter* to Fields, the publisher reported Hawthorne saying, "It is either very good or very bad, I don't know which." And later he wrote to Fields (April 13, 1854) to say of a new edition of *Mosses:* "Upon my honor, I am not quite sure that I entirely comprehend my own meaning, in some of those blasted allegories." And he could actually write of the childish *Wonder-Book* and *Tanglewood Tales* that "I never did anything else so well as these old baby stories." He was divided between profound responses to full-bodied sexuality and an intense need to repress those responses, a writer who felt compelled to work, as Frye's definition of The Romance suggests, in a medium where strange and unnatural forces were his subject, but was equally compelled in his prefatory remarks to deny his legitimate province.

In a letter to Fields concerning the sketches of England appearing in *The Atlantic Monthly,* Hawthorne speaks of his "unshakable conviction that all this series of articles is good for nothing; but that is none of my business, provided the public and you are of a different opinion." Lionel Trilling seems to me entirely correct when he asserts that Hawthorne's relation to the public of his own day was a matter of great moment in his thoughts about himself. Hawthorne seems never to have been sure whether to be ashamed or proud of his lack of success with the mass of his countrymen. And, of course, this was not merely a question of his career but of his moral life, feeling as he did that to be removed from one's fellow beings was to commit a mortal sin. Hawthorne means the adjective quite literally when he speaks of his "cursed habits of solitude." In all his work he held to the notion that isolation was a crime, yet his craft allied him against the community on the side of that crime.

Marius Bewley suggests in *The Eccentric Design* that Hawthorne's real contribution to critical writing in this country comes in his discussion of this problem of his audience: not when Hawthorne is talking about "the relation of the artist to his art, but in terms of his relation to society." Bewley feels that Hawthorne was unable "to reconcile the roles of artist and citizen in the context of American society, or to make a workable creative marriage between solitude and society."

The difficulty began early in Hawthorne's career when he was, as Poe called him, "the example, *par excellence,* in this country, of the privately-admired and publicly-unappreciated man of genius." Hawthorne continued the complaint in the voice of Aubépine: "He must necessarily find himself without an audience, except here and there an individual or possibly an isolated clique." Troubled as he was by the act of writing itself, Hawthorne found his lack of readership at the center of the problem. When did the solitude necessary for work become guilty withdrawal? No one listens. He sits alone. Is the silence out there some proof that the silence in here is the quiet of impotence? He never could get over that; in England he was persistently troubled by the dream that he was still failing, still lagging behind his classmates at school and unable to join, as they did, in the business of the American community. When he took his first breath of real success with *The Scarlet Letter,* he could look with some relief back on his early work. He now had a public. But in his preface to the third edition of *Twice-Told Tales* in 1851 he remarks that when the tales were first written he had despaired of being capable of "addressing the American public, or, indeed, any public at all."

When he had his audience, he was just as deeply in trouble of a different kind. The public, he had learned from bitter personal experience, could hiss and laugh a man down; if he were not careful they would give his writing the same treatment they had given him as a Custom-House official. When Hawthorne speaks in his own voice—in the stories or in the prefaces—he is not only a writer but also a private man who worries about what people will say of him. That other man intrudes on the action set in motion by the writer; the author of the great passages in the book is not the same Hawthorne who slides in a defensive introductory note. He writes in the preface to *Blithedale* that he does not "put forward the slightest pretensions to illustrate a theory, or elicit a conclusion, favorable or otherwise," in respect to socialism. The book elicits an unmistakable "otherwise" conclusion "in respect to socialism," but the public man would not admit it.

The famous preface to *The House of Seven Gables* is rather less than accurate about the romance itself. His story, Hawthorne says, will be filtered through a handful of "legendary mist, which the reader, according to his pleasure, may either disregard or allow it to float almost imperceptibly about the characters and events for the sake of a picturesque effect." At the end of his preface Hawthorne asks that "the book may be read strictly as a Romance, having a great deal more to do with the clouds over-head than with any portion of the actual soil of the County of Essex." But he protests too much. In the opening scene of the book this direction to heavenly territory indicates an evasion. The portrait of Matthew Maule's violent end, "a death that blasted with strange horror" his property, does not take place in "cloud-land." Hawthorne strikes out at all "those who take upon themselves to be leaders of the people" and who are "fully liable to all the passionate error that has ever characterized the maddest mob." Hawthorne's indictment of the Puritans—who massacred " their own equals, brethren, and wives"—is spelled out in an unqualified passion unusual for Hawthorne's writing in general and surely out of keeping with his prefatory description of his work as "woven of so humble a texture." At the death scene we see "clergymen, judges, statesmen—the wisest, calmest, holiest persons of their day—in the inner circle round the gallows, loudest to applaud the work of blood, latest to confess themselves miserably deceived." All this comes only three paragraphs away from the gently ironic preface, at the beginning of the story proper. Hawthorne's preface maintains a condescending attitude toward "some definite moral purpose " and wryly indicates that he does not want to be "deficient in this particular." At the beginning of the story itself, however, one feels as if someone who had been repeatedly pushed back into the wings has finally got the stage. There is no butterfly of a story being impaled on the iron rod of a moral; the story itself generates sufficient iron.

Hawthorne adopts, then, a curiously defensive and misleading tone when he addresses himself to the people he hopes will read his books. He attempts to anticipate various criticisms and find answers to them. Uncertain as to what the public might make of his work, he says that he "has proposed to himself—but with what success, fortunately, it is not for him to judge—to keep undeviatingly within his immunities." So concerned is he with keeping "within his immunities" that when he attempts to speak to a general public about matters of social concern, his voice seems drastically unsure. He hated the institution of slavery, and early in his life went on record against it. But in his *Life of Franklin Pierce* (which appeared the same year as *Blithedale*), he saw slavery as "one of those evils which divine Providence does not leave to be remedied by human contrivances, but which, in its own good time, by some means impossible to be anticipated . . . it causes to vanish like a dream." In the article "Chiefly About War Matters," which appeared in *The Atlantic Monthly* for July 1862, he wrote of John Brown: "Nobody was ever more justly hanged," and "any common-sensible man, looking at the matter unsentimentally, must have felt a certain intellectual satisfaction in seeing him hanged, if it were only in requital of his preposterous miscalculation of possibilities." At the bottom of the page, what appears to be a footnote by the editors of *The Atlantic* says: "Can it be a son of old Massachusetts who utters this abominable statement? For shame." James writes in 1879 that "the editor of the periodical appears to have thought that he must give the antidote with the poison, and the paper is accompanied with several little notes disclaiming all sympathy with the writer's political heresies." James wonders at "the questionable taste of the editorial commentary, with which it is strange that Hawthorne should have allowed his article to be encumbered." Stranger still does the whole matter appear when one discovers that "the questionable taste" was that of Hawthorne himself, for it was he who wrote out the footnote disclaimers. He says his article (printed anonymously) is written "By A Peaceable Man." He is, indeed, peaceable.

The problem is deeply involved with his sense of his audience, for during these same last years of his life he could write in a straightforward and courageous way, still capable of setting down his convictions with great force and clarity. He writes to Fields about the dedication to Franklin Pierce which he wanted to be published as a preface to *Our Old Home*. The letter replies to the effort several of his friends had made, through Fields, to keep the letter out of the book. They said that since Northern sentiment was then against the former president, the dedication would hurt the book's sales and Hawthorne's reputation. Hawthorne replies:

I find that it would be a piece of poltroonery in me to withdraw either the dedication or the dedicatory letter. My long and intimate personal relations with Pierce render the dedication altogether proper, especially as regards this book, which would have had no existence without his kindness; and if he is so exceedingly unpopular that his name is enough to sink the volume, there is so much the more need that an old friend should stand by him. I cannot, merely on account of pecuniary profit or literary reputation, go back from what I have deliberately felt and thought it right to do; and if I were to tear out the dedication, I should never look at the volume again without remorse and shame. As for the literary public, it must accept my book precisely as I see fit to give it, or let it alone.

Nevertheless, I have no fancy for making myself a martyr, when it is conscientiously possible to avoid it; and I always measure out my heroism very accurately according to the exigencies of the occasion, and should be the last man in the world to throw away a bit of it needlessly. So I have looked over the concluding paragraph and have amended it in such a way that, while doing what I know to be justice to my friend, it contains not a word that ought to be objectionable to any set of readers. If the public of the North sees fit to ostracize me for this, I can only say that I would gladly sacrifice a thousand or two of dollars rather than retain the good will of such a herd of dolts and mean-spirited scoundrels.

There are no mellowed lights or enriched shadows here. The letter is a perfect example of all that we miss in the prefaces: there is no cautionary, diffuse irony, no cloying playfulness. In his letter he has mastered those tensions between his personal sense of duty and his awareness of social demands.

Nothing shows his martyrdom to the problem more clearly than the preface to *The Marble Faun,* where he asks of the "congenial reader" he has always written for: "is he extant now?" Hawthorne wonders if he may find his old gentle reader only under "some mossy gravestone." He had before him the example of Melville, who had lost his audience and had "pretty much made up his mind to be annihilated." Hawthorne was writing in "a foreign land, and after a long, long absence from my own." Eight years earlier, in the preface to *Gables,* he had been able to make fun of those who vaccinated their stories with a moral; here he defines his purpose as "merely to write a fanciful story, evolving a thoughtful moral." Stendhal dedicated *The Charterhouse of Parma* "to the happy few," that is, to the happy few who would understand him. Similarly, Hawthorne says that he always introduces his publications with "a familiar kind of preface, addressed nominally to the Public at large, but really to a character with whom he felt entitled to use far greater freedom." Stendhal demands understanding; Hawthorne pleads for leniency.

If the prefaces are read carefully and in sequence, they show Hawthorne's growing uncertainty about what he was doing and his gradual loss of power. In the preface to *The Marble Faun* he is obsessed with his own dislocation: the complaint of "lack of materials" is the usual one, but in 1860 it is made with a loss of assurance, a sense that he has almost forgotten why the distinction had to be spelled out when he left "the real world" for his "sort of poetic or fairy precinct." Italy, he says, offers him that precinct; America has "no shadow, no antiquity, no mystery, no picturesque and gloomy wrong." But America *did* have each one of these— the shadow, the antiquity, the mystery, the supremely picturesque and gloomy wrong—when he constructed his masterpiece, *The Scarlet Letter.* The inference is unavoidable: he had not run out of materials; he had run out of his ability to organize them. In "The Custom-House" he complains that the story of Hester Prynne is too gloomy; in the preface to *The Marble Faun* he complains that his homeland is too sunshiny. In "The Custom-House" he laments his inability to get down onto the page the details of the world he was living in; a decade later he writes that his latest romance has too much stuffing of local color but, after all, "these things fill the mind everywhere in Italy, and especially in Rome, and cannot easily be kept from flowing out upon the page when one writes freely, and with self-enjoyment." Could Hawthorne say that he wrote *The Scarlet Letter* "freely and with self-enjoyment"? His great gift was the ability to make representative selection; it enabled him, in his best work, to circumscribe and bring to life the essentials of his subject. But near the end of his career he is apologizing for his inability to make the selection, for the elaboration of mere pictorial effects. What gives that apology its full tragic resonance is not only his admission that he feels his power has deserted him but also his uncertainty that anyone will listen with sympathy while he makes his declaration. "I stand upon ceremony now."

hand, has all avenues of escape cut off to him; his collapse results from his feeling of being trapped in his ministerial office where daily circumstances force on him the discrepancy between his character and his reputation. Hawthorne says of himself, "It was not the first time, nor the second that I had gone away." Salem's "flat, unvaried surface" explains his restlessness in the "tame" town; any fondness for it is like "a sentimental attachment to a disarranged checkerboard." The character of the world is not dangerous hostility but simple barrenness. Women are conspicuously absent; they have "very infrequent access" to this sterile country of old men. The aged retainers in the Custom-House are human embodiments of Salem itself: dilapidated vestiges of vitality, shells, which can only suggest, as the rotting houses do, that once there was life inside them. Hawthorne gently pokes fun at their senility: "sagaciously, under their spectacles did they peep into the holds of vessels! Mighty was their fuss about little matters." He is fond of them: "as my position in reference to them, being paternal and protective, was favorable to the growth of friendly sentiments, I soon grew to like them all." I cannot fathom some modern judgments of what is going on here; one critic writes that "the narrator's treatment of the old men suggests a vicarious form of revenge for the sense of unworthiness evoked by his ancestors. His quasi-sadistic pleasure in the old men's insecurity looks forward to Chillingworth's prolonged torture of Dimmesdale." Similarly, another reader asserts that "The Custom-House" "contains the kind of biting, sometimes gory images that sensation lovers feasted upon." Such verdicts make me wonder if we are reading the same text. Surely in his preface Hawthorne is having some fun, not engaging in "quasi-sadistic pleasure" that anticipates Chillingworth, nor indulging himself in a feast for sensation lovers of "gory images." Calling himself "decapitated," and comparing himself to "Irving's Headless Horseman" is clearly not what the critic calls "typically macabre newspaper imagery." No, Hawthorne sums up the life in his portrait of the Inspector, who is all externals and "animal nature." His food is his mentality. Indeed, with just enough spirit "to keep the old gentleman from walking on all fours," he has "no power of thought, no depth of feeling, no troublesome sensibilities." In spite of Hawthorne's defense in the second edition that the entire Custom-House sketch is remarkable only for "frank and genuine good-humor" and "general accuracy," it is easy to see why on March 21, 1850, *The Salem Register* called the portrait of the Inspector "the most venomous, malignant, and unaccountable assault." In his preface Hawthorne damns the Inspector, however humorously, as a half-man with "no soul, no heart, no mind: nothing . . . but instincts." This is no country for the man from the Old Manse; the Inspector is the one "fittest to be a Custom-House officer."

"But it is time to quit this sketch!" And, as we read on, we see Hawthorne quit not only the sketch itself but also the kind of attitude toward his subject matter that the satiric portrait involves. He turns to the Collector, who "seemed away from us, although we saw him but a few yards off; remote, though we passed close beside his chair; unattainable, though we might have stretched forth our hands and touched his own." Thus, in these two portraits Hawthorne embodies in the idiom of personality the distinction he will later make between the actual and the imaginary.

The tone of these first pages of the essay is assured irony; Hawthorne's intelligence is in firm control of the shabby world in which he is making at least a living. The issues he raises are not resounding, but they are clear. As the essay proceeds, however, the potency of the experience he deals with unsettles his pose as a man of society. As he rummages in documents, he comes upon the records of Mr. Surveyor Pue, who has left the story of Hester Prynne and the symbol of her life, the scarlet letter. Here in a "forgotten corner," Hawthorne discovers his true relation to his homeland. When he sees the apparition of the ghostly surveyor, Hawthorne speaks of "my filial duty and reverence towards him—who might reasonably regard himself as my official ancestor." Now Hawthorne understands the duality of his heritage: the Puritans of his family tree and the man who lives on the page where he has written. Immediately, Hawthorne's life work is set before him. The ghost of Surveyor Pue commands: "'I charge you, in this matter of Old Mistress Prynne, give to your predecessor's memory the credit which will be rightfully due!'" Hawthorne's Puritan forebears had bequeathed to him materials, the signs of punishment and guilt; his literary ancestor appears to assign him the task of translating those signs into art.

Although Hawthorne has made this great discovery, he has difficulty turning it into action. Even when he is away from the Custom-House, in his home and on his walks, he is despondent, erratic, and unsatisfied. His life is at loose ends. His first tendency is to find fault with the situation; he complains, "so little adapted is the atmosphere of a Custom-House to the delicate harvest of fancy and sensibility." But then he probes more deeply into his dilemma and concludes: "The fault was mine. The page of life that was spread out before me seemed dull and commonplace only because I had not fathomed its deeper import." In this Hawthorne further emphasizes and illustrates his basic method. First he locates a problem in the exterior world of fact, then locates the answer to that problem by turning inward to self-examination. He is tempted to stay on the surface, stay with the facts, not to dive into their causes and ultimately to see them in personal terms. But the details and general design of "The Custom-House" function to show Hawthorne's continual efforts to make these radical readjustments of perception.

In his famous definition of The Romance, he starts by emphasizing that the genre is neither actual nor imaginary but a meeting place where each may "imbue itself with the nature of the other." He gives us "the domestic scenery of the well-known apartment," then goes on to note how the invading moonlight changes "a child's shoe, the doll, seated in her little wicker carriage, the hobby horse," then emphasizes the importance of a dying fire to add warmth to the scene, and finally looks into the mirror on the wall, "with one more remove further from the actual, and nearer to the imaginative." In his definition Hawthorne embodies the entire movement of "The Custom-House." The effect is of both motion and rest: the gradual turning of the eye from furniture to moonlight to fire to mirror; yet the entire set piece exists as a static tableau, a miniature of a general shifting of emphasis from actual to imaginary in "The Custom-House" essay as a whole.

Hawthorne's critics have usually valued "The Custom-House" for this definition, but their abundant concern with esthetic theory has tended to obscure the moral force of the essay. Hawthorne did not happen to write allegorical romance because he had concocted the pictorial terms. His "Custom-House" definition of Romance is, mainly, charming. "Hawthorne's Charm" is not the kind of article one can find in today's literary journals; the modern critical mind will not allow itself to think in those terms. But words like "charm" and "grace" and "ethereal" were the words Hawthorne wanted us to use in thinking of his work. His little picture of The Romance shows us one part of his mind—a large part, for he plays variations on the picture in each succeeding preface to his long works of fiction. But while this room of dusky light in "The Custom-House" is artfully done, there is something finally unsatisfying about it. The discovery of the scarlet letter needed no moonlight effects to burn itself into Hawthorne's mind. He did not have to put an actual thing into an imaginative envelope; both are there contained in the cloth. When he found it, Hawthorne endeavored to see through to its imaginative reality, for it had "some deep meaning in it, most worthy of interpretation." He did not need to set the stage; the letter itself offered the meaning to his mind and the picture to his eye. The experience, as he tells it, contradicts the definition as he makes it and explains his discomfort with the definition itself. He builds a moonlit room only to discover that it cannot contain what he wants to say. He is unable to apprehend "the reality of the flitting hour . . . because my brain wanted the insight and my hand the cunning to transcribe it."

But Salem makes him take up his pen again. When the Whigs come in, Hawthorne is forced out, back to his old vocation. At the end of his essay he inverts the terms that began it. The Custom-House, which once stood for actuality and hostility to imagination, is now "a dream." The real "old native town" is "no portion of the real earth" but rather in "cloud land, with only imaginary inhabitants." All which was previously an index of the real now "ceases to be a reality of my life." Hawthorne indicates that his connection with his ancestors buried in the town is one of "sensuous sympathy of dust with dust," that is, external and physical ties. But when he finds the manuscript left by Surveyor Pue, Hawthorne says that the interest lies in the "internal operations of his head." Note, finally, the early remark that when he took his post, he "might as well or better, have gone somewhere else." If we have read carefully, that playful, casual phrase is still with us when Hawthorne makes his declaration of independence: "I am a citizen of somewhere else."

The echoic effects that operate in "The Custom-House" resonate in *The Scarlet Letter.* In his autobiographical essay Hawthorne says that he constantly returns to his native place like a "bad half-penny . . . as if Salem were for me the inevitable center of the universe." He says, "my doom was upon me." Hester Prynne's remaining in Boston is like Hawthorne returning to Salem; the same word, "doom," and the same sense of attraction is repeated: "But there is a feeling so irresistible and inevitable that it has the force of doom, which almost invariably compels human beings to linger around and haunt, ghost-like, the spot where some great and marked event has given the color to their life-time." Hawthorne, in this manner, links his own experience to Hester's. In the beginning of his introductory sketch he makes a claim of personal privilege, complete with apology and self-deprecation; a similar apology is made at the end of the essay when he introduces *The Scarlet Letter*. He adopts the same tone for himself as he does for his art. This is especially persuasive when he points out after he is "decapitated" that "there are few uglier traits of human nature than this tendency—which I now witnessed in men no worse than their neighbors—to grow cruel, merely because they possessed the power of inflicting harm." Hawthorne so bitterly documents this "fierce spirit of malice and revenge" that at the end of the preface we too are "citizens of somewhere else" because we have shared his voyage there. The solitary walks through Boston that we take with Hester Prynne begin in Salem in "The Custom-House," for Hawthorne works in it to build up in us a feeling of alienation that we will bring with us when we view Hester standing alone on the scaffold.

What gives Hawthorne's autobiographical essay its own great tension and its aptness as an introduction to *The Scarlet Letter* is this sense that the validations of the community have given way and that the individual by himself cannot adequately make meaning out of experience. In "The Devil in Manuscript," Hawthorne complains of the writer's life in the voice of his character Oberon (Hawthorne's own nickname to his close college friends): "I have become ambitious of a bubble, and careless of solid reputation. I am surrounding myself with shadows, which bewilder me, by aping the realities of life. They [his tales] have drawn me aside from the beaten path of the world, and led me into a strange sort of solitude,—a solitude in the midst of men,—where nobody wishes for what I do, nor thinks nor feels as I do." This "strange sort of solitude—a solitude in the midst of men"—is the reason for Hawthorne's distraction, and later in his novel it is the root of the terror felt by his heroine, Hester Prynne. They are both pushed back "from the beaten path of the world" and their private faculties are inadequate to interpret the signals of the world.

In "The Custom-House" and in the dark tale that follows it, Hawthorne's manner and subject proceed from his sense of how the American community fails and frustrates the impulses of creative people by forcing them back too much upon themselves. We can, then, immediately feel the isolation of Hester Prynne: we have lived through the progressive stages of it in her author's life. In "The Custom-House" Hawthorne authenticates the emotional reality of Hester's story just as he authenticates the physical, historical reality when he discovers the scarlet A.

When at the end of his essay Hawthorne assesses *The Scarlet Letter,* he complains that it has "a stern and somber aspect; too much ungladdened by genial sunshine; too little relieved by the tender and familiar." It presents "an uncaptivating effect." He looks at his work in much the same way that his character Oberon reacted to his writing: "He drew the tales towards him, with a mixture of natural affection and natural disgust, like a father taking a deformed infant into his arms." The page is what his passion made, but now that it exists there in its own right, the creator cannot quite recognize it as his own; what he does recognize is that part of himself which he has so often tried to restrain. Hawthorne was deeply troubled by the knowledge that *The Scarlet Letter* was no passport back to the land of community. The local indignation when "The Custom-House" was published only reinforced the feeling of alienation when it was written. Hawthorne expressed his reaction to the outrage in Salem in a letter to his friend Horatio Bridge, April 13: "If I escape from town without being tarred and feathered, I shall consider it good luck. I wish they would tar and feather me; it would be such an entirely novel kind of distinction for a literary man. And, from such judges as my fellow-citizens, I should look upon it as a higher honor than a laurel crown." When at the opening of "The Custom-House" he thought of his ancestors, he remembered William Hathorne and his son John, one of the three judges at the Salem witchcraft trials in 1692. These were men distinguished by public activity, and, indeed, Hawthorne defines them only by their official capacities. But when he finds those documents of Mr. Surveyor Pue, he notes that they were "not official, but of a private nature." Subsequently Hawthorne turns from official, public activities in The Custom-House to private writing. This latter work, he says, may receive either neglect or censure from the community. Thus, his obsession with the guilt that his ancestors incurred in public places becomes for him transformed into a new feeling of guilt at his failure to take part in the work of his community. The writing of "story books" is not simply a job that the venerable forebears would have ridiculed: art involves, in Hawthorne's mind, a kind of social irresponsibility. He felt the imperative to "stand in some true relation with his audience." The writing of fiction, he knew, might be not only a solitary but also a subversive job; its validity would be tested by its contribution to the community. But finally he discovered that, while "it has been as dear an object as any in my literary efforts" to be "of some importance" to the townspeople, they "will do just as well without me." That situation violated the moral imperative he most frequently stated and deeply held.

Hawthorne fought hard to keep his Salem job; in later years he was to try government work again as writer in a presidential campaign and in the consulship at Liverpool. But he wrote his greatest book when he had just experienced severe condemnation, when he had just seen lifeless standardization. He calls his introductory papers "posthumous"; they mark the death of any confidence he had that he could trust the community to validate his labor. Only in *The Scarlet Letter* itself was Hawthorne able to make a form adequate to the magnitude of the problems raised in "The Custom-House." But his insistence on getting his Salem experiences into print with the story of Boston—even after the original idea that the volume should include several shorter tales and sketches had been abandoned—indicates how closely the two times were linked in his mind. The personal record and the historical romance together show that Hawthorne is too stern to accept the values of his fellow citizens, too stern, even, to dismiss them easily. Although he had grave reservations about making passage to "the realm of quiet," he was impelled to stand, in 1850, absolutely there.

Chapter Five

The Tongue of Flame

Sigmund Freud was not (so far as I know) thinking about *The Scarlet Letter* when he wrote *Civilization and Its Discontents*. But a brief paragraph from Freud's book can be applied with accuracy and force to the history of Hester Prynne in Puritan Boston:

> Human life in communities only becomes possible when a number of men unite together in strength superior to any single individual and remain united against all single individuals. The strength of this united body is then opposed as "Right" against the strength of any individual, which is condemned as "brute force." This substitution of the power of a united number for the power of a single man is the decisive step towards civilization. The essence of it lies in the circumstance that the members of the community have restricted their possibilities of gratification whereas the individual recognized no such restrictions. The first requisite of culture, therefore, is justice—that is, the assurance that a law once made will not be broken in favor of any individual.

Hawthorne wrote *The Scarlet Letter* with great speed, often working over nine hours a day. Henry James said, "the subject had probably lain a long time in his mind." Indeed it had: for over a decade Hawthorne had

Hester Prynne, after a painting by Jared Flagg.
Courtesy, Division of Rare and Manuscript Collections,
Carl A. Kroch Library, Cornell University.

pondered a slowly ripening image, a scarlet letter, A, on a woman's bodice. In "Endicott and the Red Cross" (1837) he had asked us to see

> a young woman, with no mean share of beauty, whose doom it was to wear the letter A on the breast of her gown, in the eyes of all the world and her own children. And even her own children knew what the initial signified. Sporting with her infamy, the lost and desperate creature had embroidered the fatal token in scarlet cloth, with golden thread and the nicest art of needlework, so that the capital A might have been thought to mean Admirable, or anything rather than Adulteress.

When he was forced out of his job at the Salem Custom-House, Hawthorne picked up that letter again; now he was ready to invest the symbol with its full power.

We should remember that from early on he had had in mind both the starkness of the brand and the luxuriance of the embroidery. In almost Miltonic stately cadences—"Sporting with her infamy the lost / And desperate creature"—the golden thread says adultery is beautiful, says Right you are, and richer than you know!

Hawthorne mentions the letter, on average, more than once every two pages. The modulations he plays on the A are not always successful, and when he talks of its lurid gleam and magical properties he stumbles. The superhuman badge that protects Hester from Indian arrows, the flaming A in the night sky—these are examples of Hawthorne's burdening a meaningful symbol with distracting and overwrought effects. These errors are open enough and sufficiently commented upon, but something may still be said about the way the A focuses our attention on the central issues Hawthorne confronts in Puritan Boston.

First of all, we must take it literally. Critics have been overly ingenious, telling us that the A stands not only for Adultery and Able but also for Art, America, and Arthur. No. As John Thompson has written, "the title truly is *The Scarlet Letter*, and it is truly about sex: about what happens to our sex in the condition of American culture." Hawthorne, skittish at first (skittish as always), worried about the lurid quality of *Scarlet*, and suggested that perhaps *The Judgment Letter* might be a better title. But then, persuaded by the other side of his temperament, he suggested that the title be printed in flaming red on the cover of the book. The scarlet A is the ideal mythic type of the portion of the American past that he was exploring, the least far-fetched symbol he could have used to tell this story of Massachusetts. Historically grounded, pictorially vivid, the letter calls into play the central impulses of the colony. Yvor Winters has written that "in the setting which Hawthorne chose, allegory was realism, the idea was life itself." Hawthorne's "inveterate love of allegory," his desire constantly to work with symbolic signs rather than experiential particulars, here is turned into a chief merit of his writing style and not a temperamental defect. The A is the focal point not just for our eyes; it embodies where the Puritans were and who they were and why they lived as they did. The A becomes, in Kenneth Burke's phrase, "the informing anecdote," the one resonant symbol which carries with it all that the story will reveal. In chapter 15, "Hester and Pearl," we read that "as the last touch to her mermaid's garb, Pearl took some eel-grass, and imitated, as best she could, on her own bosom, the decoration with which she was so familiar on her mother's. A letter,— the letter A,—but freshly green, instead of scarlet!" Three times Pearl asks, "What does the letter mean, mother?" And finally Hester answers, "Silly Pearl, what questions are these? There are many things in this world that a child must not ask about," and she resonantly concludes, "as for the scarlet letter, I wear it for the sake of its gold thread!" Exactly. And, as I said, the "gold thread" is not something else, or something that happens later. The gold thread is there from the very beginning, an essential, virtually instinctual part of the larger plan. Punitive scarlet and celebratory gold. Those two. That one.

In choosing the image Hawthorne made the greatest choice of his writing life; never again would he find that single dramatic and coherent symbol around which to build a fiction. The furry ears of Donatello in *The Marble Faun,* for example, are in no way "the informing anecdote" of that book and are curiously inadequate as a vehicle for the questions the book raises. But the scarlet letter raises a very great question: by what signs shall ye know them? The business of the book is to elaborate the A, to put it in different terms. The letter stands as a brutally clear meaning, but since it is only a letter, the heroine may change by her actions the word in which the letter belongs. She has already done so when we meet her; she has made "a pride of what they, worthy gentlemen, meant for a punishment."

In the first scene Hester stands there, an emblem of sin. The Puritan community has designed the letter to erase the sinner, to obliterate her individuality. She is supposed to be the general symbol of "woman's sinful passion." But Hawthorne keeps taking us into Hester's "inward sphere" behind the letter to show us the discrepancy between what the community can see and who Hester is. Thus, the reality that society has defined provides the fighting terms of the book: either the meaning assigned by the community will retain its repressive function or it will yield through the efforts of the central character to a new meaning. Hester's embroidery has already begun to answer the question; it is the visible sign that she has taken her place and will endure it with a vengeance.

Hawthorne had already jotted down in his notebook, in capital letters, "A Secret Thing In Public." It is a perfect description of the scarlet letter. That is who Hester is, when we first see her trapped, helpless and lonely on the pillory undergoing the censure of the assembled townspeople. All they do is look at her in silent punishment. Or, as D. H. Lawrence flamboyantly claimed, the citizens of Boston are really worshipping Hester as the incarnation of their forbidden desires.

Whatever way you look at it, there is a dark feeling of despair and loss, something extremely strange in the air of mid-nineteenth-century New England. Hawthorne's great neighbors, Emerson and Thoreau, were busy proclaiming "the infinitude of the private man." Walt Whitman was very soon to proclaim the United States itself "the greatest poem." But Hawthorne's tragic heroine is constantly confined by American society, entrapped and tortured by the massive *fact* of it. Her story bleakly contradicts the prevailing optimism of the day, as do her essential life and most telling gestures.

She is radically unlike the stereotypic heroines in the popular literature of 1850. Oliver Wendell Holmes found her a profound relief from the "languid, lifeless, sexless creations" he usually encountered in American novels. Hester Prynne is an absolutely astonishing figure in nineteenth-century New England culture, a woman whose character is a direct expression of her powerful sexuality. Her very existence is rooted in the community's recognition of her sexual independence. She is a "Fallen Woman"—a "Dark Lady"—who generates moral and intellectual strength from her defiant refusal to accept the masculine world's definition of her. She surrounds the stigmatizing "A" on the breast of her gown with the "gorgeous luxuriance of elaborate embroidery." "Gorgeous" in 1850 meant not only "dazzlingly beautiful or magnificent," as in today's usage, but in that chaster day it signified "overly sumptuous," with implications of sexual irregularity and sensual "indulgence."

Twice in the novel Ann Hutchinson is mentioned, and Hester walks in her "footsteps." Over twenty years earlier Hawthorne had written in his biographical sketch of Mistress Hutchinson, "In the midst, and in the center of all eyes, we see the woman. She stands loftily before her judges with a determined brow; and unknown to herself, there is a flash of carnal pride half-hidden in her eye, as she surveys the many learned and famous men whom her doctrines have put in fear." Such a description could go straight into *The Scarlet Letter* (with perhaps the exception of "doctrines," though even that is applicable by the end).

Hester "had in her nature a rich, voluptuous, oriental characteristic—a taste for the gorgeously beautiful" ("gorgeous" again, and this time "oriental"). Moreover, she is not just physically brilliant; she is "brilliant" in the sense of "bright"—she has an active, alert, imaginative mind. She may think wrongly at times, but she thinks more profoundly than anyone else. And most importantly Hawthorne sees her far more clearly than his other brilliant heroines; we don't sense any mystification about her sin, and she is not distorted by deep, unsolved secrets. She *is* a deep and unsolved secret. Hawthorne does not encumber her with gimmicky curses as he does Miriam and Beatrice or tacked-on charges as he does Zenobia.

Hester's first act in the story is one of rebellion; led out of the dark prison by the town beadle, "she repelled him by an act marked with natural dignity and force of character, and stepped into the open air, as if by her own free will." The book marks dramatic confrontations between Hester and those who would repress her. When the judges try to take her daughter away from her, she confronts "the old Puritan magistrate with almost a fierce expression" showing that "she felt that she possessed indefeasible rights against the world, and she was ready to defend them to the death." From the very beginning, when Hester not only bears the letter but brandishes it, "The world's law was no law for her mind." At the end, when Dimmesdale ascends the scaffold to make his public confession, Hester draws near "slowly, as if impelled by inevitable fate and against her strongest will." She is reluctant; she does not want him in the market-place, she does not want him under terms of the "world's law."

For Hester, from the very start of the story, experience is over. It is not to have. The world has been turned around. The future is the past. The world has told her she is no longer allowed to be a woman. But she knows that what the world tells her is false; her love for Dimmesdale and for her daughter proves to her daily that she is a woman. On the scaffold, when she faces the multitude, "she was supported by an unnatural tension of the nerves, and by all the combative energy of her character, which enabled her to convert the scene into a kind of lurid triumph." That lurid triumph cannot last, for the intensity of the mad moment of public display must be borne out in dreary routine: "with the unattended walk from her prison-door began the daily custom; and she must either sustain and carry it forward by the ordinary resources of her nature, or sink beneath it." Hester endures the knowledge that no one will respond to her as Hester but "as the figure, the body, the reality of sin." Women are the only people who feel a common twinge, a sense of shame, when they see the scarlet letter. Men notice it and know what it stands for—although Indians and Governor Bellingham's manservant think that it stands for high rank. Hester comes to have a "dread of children" because "the utterance of a word that had no distinct purport to their own minds, but was none the less terrible to her as proceeding from lips that babbled it unconsciously. It seemed to argue so wide a diffusion of her shame, that all nature knew of it." In her walks with Pearl she has to face children and hear them say, "Come, let us fling mud at them."

From the beginning, when she tries to conceal the sign of adultery with the product of adultery, she fights back. In another sense, she simply takes the world on its own terms; she plays the role her culture assigns to her. And by behaving herself she becomes "Able." She is given "a part to perform in the world." Humble in that sense, at least, she continues to display her vibrant sexuality and deep inner resources. Anthony Trollope, in an article for *The North American Review,* wrote that in *The Scarlet Letter* "the reader is expected to sympathize with the woman—and will sympathize only with her." She has, as even Chillingworth says, "great elements."

When Hawthorne wrote of women, he usually tended to divide them, as has so often been remarked upon, into two groups: the blondes and the brunettes, the light snow maidens and the dark women of voluptuous nature and high passion. Of the snow maidens Emily Dickinson would later exclaim, "What soft cherubic creatures / These gentlewomen are!" In a little sketch, "The Canal Boat," Hawthorne indicates his distaste for the American idea of women; he speaks of "the pure, modest, sensitive, and shrinking women of America—shrinking when no evil is intended, and sensitive like diseased flesh, that thrills if you but point at it." Hawthorne does not always stick by this indictment; his creation of Phoebe and Priscilla and Hilda shows that he, too, was enamored of "the pure, modest, sensitive, and shrinking woman of America." But he did have a love of vitality and rich sexuality. "As a point of taste," he wrote that he would prefer his dove-ladies to the English matrons he described in *Our Old Home,* but, he said, "it is a pity that we must choose between a greasy animal and an anxious skeleton."

The interesting thing in *The Scarlet Letter,* in this regard, is the way he plays with the conventions of hero and heroine, suggesting in his play a criticism of the American stereotypes of sexual roles. In Old Boston the roles are reversed. T. Walter Herbert correctly calls Hester Prynne "a manly woman and Arthur Dimmesdale a womanly man." Dimmesdale's sin never really feels like seduction; Hester seems more the seducer than the seduced. Hester Prynne is the first real woman in American literature and still the greatest. Hawthorne piles superlatives about her: "none so ready as she is to give," "none so self-devoted as Hester," "unfailing to every real demand, and inexhaustible by the largest."

Dimmesdale, on the other hand, is not the dashing, decisive young pastor; he is constantly described in the language normally applied to the young maiden heroines of the sentimental novels. He compulsively holds his hand over his heart the way the persecuted dove-ladies compulsively put the backs of their white hands to their white brows. Dimmesdale is a damsel in distress. In the forest scene he begs Hester for help: "Be thou strong for me!" "Advise me what to do." "I am powerless to go!" "Think for me, Hester! Thou art strong. Resolve for me!" These are the words scattered out by snow maidens to their swashbuckling saviors in Brockden Brown and Cooper and the popular stage melodramas. In *The Scarlet Letter* Hawthorne has turned about completely not only the general nature of the hero–heroine conventions in mid-nineteenth-century fiction, but he also has turned around the whole complex of tags and devices and stock poses that went along with those conceptions.

Hester keeps asking, "What is this being which I have brought into the world!" "Is that my Pearl?" Pearl, in turn, becomes a cameo of Hester; looking at herself in a salty pool of tidewater, she soon finds "that either she or the image was unreal." Hester asks Pearl what the A means. Pearl answers, "It is the great letter A. Thou hast taught me in the hornbook." "A" is the first letter the child learned, and she learned it in a context appropriate for understanding what it means on her mother's bosom:

A

> In Adam's fall
> we sinnéd all.

Language and sin are inseparable on Hester's breast. "A" is the first letter and the letter from which all others follow. On Hester's dress it signals sexual irregularity; it is thus associated with the first sin which forced man and woman out of the garden and from which all sins follow. The A, then, is at the beginning of things in our minds, the first sin which infects all subsequent society and the first verbal signal we learn in order to communicate in society.

The scarlet letter is a sign of the times. It covers and announces the bosom, standing on "that inward sphere." As the novel unfolds, the letter becomes what Richard Chase calls "the Hawthorne image: a cultural image of sexual love and moral community." It is that "Secret Thing In Public." Private impulse is given public articulation as a symbol of sexual shame.

While it is true that from its first publication *The Scarlet Letter* was hailed as an American classic, some of its earliest readers were dismayed. My own favorite is a scandalized custodian of culture who cried out, in *The Church Review*, "Is the French era actually begun in our literature?" The influential Orestes Brownson declared that

> Hawthorne can hardly be said to pervert God's gifts, or to exert an immoral influence. Yet his work is far from being unobjectionable. It is a story of crime, an adulteress and her accomplice. Crimes like the one

imagined are not fit subjects for popular literature, and moral health is not promoted by leading the imagination to dwell on them. There is an unsound state of public morals when the novelist is permitted, without a scorching rebuke, to select such crimes, and invest them with all the fascinations of genius and all the charms of highly polished style. No man has the right to love another man's wife, and no married woman has the right to love any man but her husband.

Nowadays we tend to think we've grown out of that prudery. What's all this fuss about Adultery? Big deal. Hester Prynne and Arthur Dimmesdale don't seem to modern readers to have "sinned," and to insist that they did only illustrates Mencken's wonderful definition of Puritanism as "the haunting suspicion that somewhere someone may be happy."

In any age, though, *The Scarlet Letter* is decidedly a gloomy book. Henry James said, "no story of love was surely ever less of a 'love-story.' " And Hawthorne himself complained that "it wears, to my eye, a stern and somber aspect, too much ungladdened by genial sunshine." He attributed that quality to "the still seething turmoil" he felt when he was writing it. He had been fired from his job in the Salem Custom-House, a victim of the spoils system, a Democrat turned out by the Whig victory of 1848. The loss of his position embittered him and created disorder in his professional and personal circumstances. His heart was broken by another, deeper loss: his beloved mother had just died. Her death caused him to break down—in public, on one occasion, the only time on record that Hawthorne experienced that kind of collapse. He wrote *The Scarlet Letter* in a desperate frenzy of sustained composition unmatched in his previous writing life.

In *Hawthorne, Melville, and the Novel*, Richard H. Brodhead remarks that "Chillingworth's free thinking is as a 'window thrown open' to Dimmesdale and shortly after this is said the two men look out of an actual open window." Brodhead argues cogently that such metaphors and actualities—side by side or fused into one—are typical of the book: "Hester embroiders robes for occasions of state, and official ceremonies like the Election Day pageant are called the 'brilliant embroidery to the great robe of state.' It is all but impossible to isolate an item in *The Scarlet Letter* that does not make both physical and metaphorical appearances." They are "manifest now as parts of an actual scene, now as features of the mind."

Brodhead cites the great forest interview between Hester and Dimmesdale as an encounter in an actual geographical place and as metaphor: Hawthorne has already spoken of "the moral wilderness in which Hester had been so long wandering." The forest appears, Brodhead asserts, as "both a natural place and as an externalization of their mental states. Our experience in the world of this novel is akin to Hawthorne's own in the moonlit room." Ordinary boundaries become fluid so that "things are seen both as facts and as thoughts."

The letter itself is designed, first by the judges and then by Hester's elaborate needlework, to be seen. The name of the book asks us to see. The chapter titles—"Another View of Hester," "The Interview," "The Interior of a Heart," "The Minister in a Maze"—all of them constantly remind us that the important question in the novel is this: how can one know a fact and at the same time see its meaning? The images of mirrors and pools and spectators predominate. When he sees his wife and another man's child, Chillingworth says to his guide, " 'Ah!'—'Aha!'—'I conceive you.' " Is that a pun on "conceive"? Michael Colacurcio is absolutely convincing when he reads what he calls "the heretical-idea-as-illegitimate-child conceit"; Colacurcio cries out, "behold the Puritan wit," in tracts that speak of an "erroneous gentlewoman herself, convicted of holding about *thirty* monstrous births at once" and "there were no more monstrous *births* than what is frequent for women laboring with *false conceptions* to produce." In these terms Hester Prynne *is* Ann Hutchinson.

A continuous theme in the book is the discrepancy between what Puritans design and the way nature refutes them. Where everything means, nothing is. For all its allegory, *The Scarlet Letter* enforces a world of anti-allegory. The elders try to locate sin, fasten it as a sign—that is their way of caging it. But like the grass growing back in the wheel tracks of the road, nature "refutes" man's arguments. The Puritans are more systematic and more intelligent than their Utopian great-grandchildren whom Hawthorne describes in *The Blithedale Romance,* but both communities, in their single-mindedness, fail. The world contradicts all schemes that do not reckon with its complexity. The Blithedalers attack evil by ignoring it; they try to reduce "the inward sphere" to an inane innocence. The Puritan community has a far deeper awareness of the power of human impulses, but the rigidity of their method fails to deal humanely with perceived error. We see the Puritan community "putting on, for ceremonials of pomp and state, the garments that had been wrought by Hester's sinful hands. Her needle-work was seen on the ruff of the Governor; military men wore it on their scarfs, and the minister on his band; it decked the baby's little cap; it was shut up, to be mildewed and moulder away in the coffins of the dead."

Hester's handiwork is in the clothes of all public and private ceremonies (except, of course, bridal veils). The "type of sin" leaves her mark on all the functions of the colony that had denied her her existence as a person. Although the letter is designed to estrange Hester from the community, it gives her a special sense of the secret sins of others, a kind of clairvoyance about the inner lives of the people around her. Thus, the stigmatizing element in sin becomes associated with increased knowledge, increased power of vision. "The tendency of her fate and fortune had been to set her free. The scarlet letter was her passport into regions where other women dared not tread." Thus, "the truth" of her situation is a language of travel complete with that prominent "passport" as she moves from state to state. In his portrait of Dimmesdale, Hawthorne repeats the figure and exclaims "A bitter kind of knowledge that!" A bitter kind for Hawthorne because the rhetoric of his book invites us to form the conclusion that sin acquaints the sinner with the knowledge that purity cannot have. *Felix culpa!* Hester wonders whether "if the truth were everywhere to be shown, a scarlet letter would blaze forth on many a bosom besides Hester Prynne's." She could, indeed, cry out a modulation of Minister Hooper's dying wail: Lo, everywhere, on every breast, a red A. In this sense the scarlet letter signifies a collapse of meaning. It is a social sign designed to perform a single function. When Hawthorne writes that it "had not done its office" he is referring, specifically, to the state of Hester's unrepentant mind. But in a more general sense the statement can be applied to the inability of the signs devised by the Puritans to perform their offices. Hawthorne continually refers to the way in which all acts reverberate in the public mind; the story is full of phrases like "no sensible men, it was confessed, could doubt" and "a widely diffused opinion" and "the vulgar idea." Hawthorne keeps showing us that although these signs are continually interpreted, the result is not density of meaning but accumulation of contrary meanings.

The quest is spelled out in agony. At the very beginning, when Hester clutches the baby to her, it screams; we are pulled into that instinctive grasp: our eyes are not down on the ground with the onlookers. Hawthorne pulls us up onto the scaffold to share the agony of Hester when she realizes "Yes!—these were her realities,—all else had vanished!" What Hester plays out publicly on the scaffold, Dimmesdale plays out in private at his mirror. He asks, "Then, what was he?—a substance?—or the dimmest of all shadows?" The search for identity is articulated in the pain of self-inquisition. "I, your pastor, whom you so reverence and trust, am utterly a pollution and a lie!" Dimmesdale is lost between what he appears to the community and what he knows is true of himself. Consequently, "the whole universe is false,—it is impalpable,—it shrinks to nothing within his grasp. And he himself, in so far as he shows himself in a false light, becomes a shadow, or, indeed, ceases to exist." These were his realities—all else had vanished.

Calvinism, Hawthorne suggests in "Young Goodman Brown," forced on its adherents the kind of morbidity and fascination with sin that made them peculiarly susceptible to temptation. And, as Hawthorne presents it, the Puritan mind is incapable of making a crucial distinction: the sinner becomes reducible to the sin. Hester is a perfect "example." The community tries to shut Hester up in a dark closet and stamp a label on the door, to obliterate herself behind her sin. That is what happens literally and allegorically in one of the finest images of the book: in Governor Bellingham's manse she sees herself reflected in a suit of armor: "the scarlet letter was represented in exaggerated and gigantic proportions, so as to be greatly the most prominent feature of her appearance. In truth, she seemed absolutely hidden behind it." Mission accomplished. The community makes of the errant woman a hideous and intolerable allegory. Denied her right to be, everywhere she must mean, must signify her sin, must be "absolutely hidden behind it."

Hester looks at her bodice and asks herself: by *these* signs you shall know me? No one is supposed to know her as a person. She must present herself to the community with a kind of doubleness (red letter and gold thread) but never as her richly various self. She can stand on the scaffold as an adulteress enduring punishment or as a prideful refutation of her judges, but she is not allowed to stand there as Hester Prynne. When she comes out of prison, the townspeople note the "desperate recklessness of her mood, by its wild and picturesque peculiarity." What they mistake is her extreme state of mind for the woman herself—all eyes focus on "the letter."

Hester is a great refutation of the Puritan mind; she brings into the community a kind of vitality which Puritanism is too narrow to contain. They refuse to express sexual passion; she incarnates it. She stands like a queen facing a mob: "tall," with "perfect elegance," "on a large scale with dark and abundant hair, so glossy that it threw off the sunshine with a gleam." She is "beautiful from regularity of feature and richness of complexion." She is "lady-like" with "feminine gentility," possessing "a certain state and dignity." She is Elizabethan largesse. The Puritans have had to delimit human variety and vitality to the point where they refuse to recognize the power of the passions which Hester incarnates. She is too much for them. What they have gained in narrowing for control they have lost in being able to cope with the most richly endowed member of the community. Thoreau wrote that the Puritans were unable to worship in the vibrant colors of an autumn forest; when the Puritans made their churches they cut down any riotous trees that would distract them from grey piety.

A second indication Hawthorne gives us of the Puritan mind's incapacity to deal with transgressors is that the mind is, in one sense, promiscuous. Why are the townspeople's eyes "fastened" on the prison door? What expectations have the public officials created in the citizenry? From the assemblage one knows that "some awful business is at hand." But, Hawthorne tells us, the members of that assemblage did not know whether they were there to see the punishment of "an undutiful child," or the driving into the forest of a "riotous Indian," or the censure of a "witch" who will "die upon the gallows," or the correction of "a sluggish bond-servant," or "an Antinomian," or a "Quaker." The Puritan mind is profoundly aware of evil, but it is incapable of discriminating among types and degrees of evil. Whatever may happen, "there was very much the same solemnity of demeanor on the part of the spectators." The Puritan does not solve a moral problem; he stamps it out.

As the beadle leads Hester onto the pillory, he shouts, "A blessing on the righteous colony of Massachusetts, where iniquity is dragged out into the sunshine!" The Puritans turn a merciless, brilliant light on sin, but the sun shines indiscriminately on all sins alike.

> Out of the whole human family, it would not have been easy to select the same number of wise and virtuous persons, who should be less capable of sitting in judgment on an erring woman's heart, and disentangling its mesh of good and evil, than the sages of rigid aspect towards whom Hester Prynne now turned her face.

Nowhere else does Hawthorne more fully explore the causes and consequences of the rigid mind than in *The Scarlet Letter*, where he makes it stand for the way society as a whole conducts its business of dealing with the isolated, mutinous individual.

The dismal severity of "the Puritanic code" is, for Hawthorne, in some sense good: it gives a coherent and deep meaning to every human act. The Puritan community takes sin with admirable seriousness. Hawthorne admires the dignity the Puritans give to human life. He finds greatness in the Puritan community: "They had fortitude and self-reliance, and, in time of difficulty or peril, stood up for the welfare of the state like a line of cliffs against a tempestuous tide." In "Main Street" he said that the Puritans "were stern, severe, intolerant, but not superstitious, not even fanatical; and endowed, if any men of that age were, with a far seeing worldly sagacity." While Hawthorne indicts the Puritans for their errors, he knows that their mind accomplished "so much, precisely because it imagined and hoped so little." They were facing almost impossible odds in a new, savage land, with little protection and little skill to fight the elements. In many cases they had to act as "one man" because the alternative was death. Hawthorne is especially attracted to Governor Bellingham, who, while he is a stern magistrate, is also able to wear a "loose gown and easy cap," to surround himself with "appliances of worldly enjoyment." The Governor's house had "a very cheery aspect; the walls being overspread with a kind of stucco, in which fragments of broken glass were plentifully intermixed; so that, when the sunshine fell aslant-wise over the front of the edifice, it glittered and sparkled as if diamonds had been flung against it by the double handful. The brilliancy might have befitted Aladdin's palace, rather than the mansion of a grave old Puritan ruler." Hawthorne says that "it is an error to suppose that our grave forefathers" simply "made it a matter of conscience to reject such means of comfort, or even luxury, as lay fairly within their grasp." The Reverend Wilson "never taught" such a creed; he "had a long-established and legitimate taste for all good and comfortable things." Hawthorne quickly points out that Wilson's "professional contemporaries" did not display with such "genial benevolence" this fullness of being. Nevertheless, Hawthorne provides us with these figures of Bellingham and Wilson so as not to reduce his portrait of the society to caricature. And, while the Puritans lacked the ability to address "the whole human brotherhood in the heart's native language," they did establish civilization on a savage continent; they did order that civilization so that it could endure. And that, surely, is the reason the setting of the book is of such stark necessity for a story of conflict between the individual and society. It was in the Puritan settlement that American society exacted its highest price; if the community was going to live at all, it would live at tremendous cost to the individual. *The Scarlet Letter* embodies Hawthorne's ambivalence about the Puritans as he expressed it in "Main Street": "Let us thank God for having given us such ancestors; and let each successive generation thank Him, not less fervently, for being one step further from them in the march of ages." The statement is a poised declaration of the attitude that informs *The Scarlet Letter*; in the novel there is a careful division of allegiances.

One prominent sign of that division is a series of cross-cultural references. Hawthorne compares the Puritan community of the past to his own present. The Puritans usually win the laurels. In a little review of Bunyan's "The Life and Death of Mr. Badman," which Hawthorne wrote for *The American Magazine of Useful and Entertaining Knowledge,* he says, "We doubt whether the present generation has not lost more than it has gained, by the philosophy which teaches it to laugh, rather than tremble, at such tales as these." In *The Scarlet Letter* Hawthorne frequently asks if the Puritans were not, far from being merely cruel, more honest and serious about human problems than his own contemporaries. Some of his commentary may seem ambiguous: the punishment of Hester Prynne was "a penalty, which in our days would infer a degree of mocking infamy and ridicule, might then be invested with almost as stern a dignity as the punishment of death itself." Is mocking infamy better or worse than the stern dignity associated with the death penalty? Hawthorne answers when he says that the scene of Hester's punishment "must always invest the spectacle of guilt and shame in a fellow-creature, before society shall have grown corrupt enough to smile, instead of shuddering, at it." Constantly these cultural cross-references appear in *The Scarlet Letter*, of a popular superstition about Hester's letter, Hawthorne says that there was "more truth in the rumor than our modern incredulity may be inclined to admit." "The discipline of the family, in those days, was of a far more rigid kind than now." Hawthorne does not dismiss the Puritans as a gloomy band; they were still invested with the old spirit of Merry England, "the offspring of sires who had known how to be merry." They were, Hawthorne suggests, capable of more merriment than his own contemporaries. Only the immediate posterity of the first settlers, "the generation next to the early emigrants," was the generation which "so darkened the national visage" that "we have yet to learn again the forgotten art of gayety."

In public places we see men of iron rigidity and women as rotundity. "The women who were now standing about the prison-door stood within less than half a century of the period when the man-like Elizabeth had been the not altogether unsuitable representative of the sex." The sun shines on "broad shoulders and well-developed busts, and on round and ruddy cheeks, that had ripened in the far-off island, and had hardly yet grown paler or thinner in the atmosphere of New England." In these cross-cultural references, we see Hawthorne indicating that the Puritan community, whatever its great errors, still had a vitality that was missing from the New England world of his own day. One female spectator to the punishment of Hester Prynne asks, "What think ye, gossips?" Another answers that the magistrates are "merciful overmuch" and "at the very least, they should have put the brand of a hot iron on Hester Prynne's forehead. Madam Hester would have winced at that, I warrant me." From the other wing of the crowd, a frightened man cries out, "Mercy on us, goodwife, is there no virtue in woman, save what springs from a wholesome fear of the gallows?" Of course there is. In the syrupy fiction of Hawthorne's contemporaries, the virtuous woman was always in bed, her single one.

There are no social situations in *The Scarlet Letter*. Relationships between people are driven to two extremes. On one hand, there are large public or ceremonial confrontations in the marketplace or the governor's manse where people are forced into categories (as the object lesson of sin or the defendant in a formal trial). On the other, there are scenes between just two or three persons, scenes in which private life becomes unbearable, since language has to carry between the two people all the emotion that has been submerged and can find release only in meetings that occur at wide intervals in time. There is no possibility for the development of a tradition of manners, for manners are not needed in this world. How could anyone say or do anything in "bad taste"? You are right or wrong, saved or damned. The one great release and efflorescence of submerged emotion in the book comes in the single, primitive social scene where the family has a brief, heretical reality: Hester, Dimmesdale, and Pearl in the forest.

In such a world Hawthorne worked confidently. He explored the region that Emerson, in *Society and Solitude,* located "underneath our domestic and neighborly life," where some "tragic necessity" is at work "driving each adult soul as with whips into the desert, and making our warm covenants sentimental and momentary." Through that place one goes down, Emerson says, "to a depth where society itself originates and disappears; where the question is, Which is first, man or men? where the individual is lost in his source." "The Prison Door" opens the book. Hawthorne calls the prison "the black flower of civilized society." In the opening chapter the war of Hawthorne's roses is between this "black flower" of civilization and the "wild rose-bush" of untamed nature. Symbolically, these flowers represent, respectively, the planned social order and the visible assertion of natural forces. The colors used in the description of the flowers impel the reader to identify the dismal flower with the soberly dressed community and the red rose with the fancifully embroidered A on Hester's bosom. When The Reverend Wilson asks Pearl who made her, the girl replies "that she had not been made at all, but had been plucked by her mother off the bush of wild roses that grew by the prison door." Pearl is usually right about these matters; in the economy of *The Scarlet Letter* she is metaphorically correct that she was born out of the passions that Hawthorne symbolizes by the red flower. The tension in the novel is between red flower and black prison, between natural impulse and repressive social force.

In exploring how this tension was organized in a people for whom "religion and law were almost identical," Hawthorne concentrates not on the theology but on its social manifestations. Hawthorne had not studied Edwards; he had read the Mathers more for history than theology. If religion and law are identical, our only way of apprehending that identity is in the way social organization expresses religious conviction. There is little disputation in the book about religious matters, no description of a church, no scene staged in one. It is the scaffold, not the church, that stands in the center of Boston. At the scaffold, where punishments are borne, we find the "congregation." Hawthorne is explicit about his charge against this congregation: "There can be no outrage, methinks, against our common nature—whatever be the delinquencies of the individual—no outrage more flagrant than to forbid the culprit to hide his face for shame, as it was the essence of this punishment to do so." The scarlet capital A is a verdict which Hawthorne issues against the community: it is the most "flagrant outrage that civilization can employ."

After noting in a newspaper that an opera was being based on *The Scarlet Letter,* Hawthorne wrote in his English notebooks that he thought "it might possibly succeed as an opera, though it would certainly fail as a play." This seems to me a remarkably keen insight into the nature of his work and its formal properties. Hawthorne knew he worked best with the isolated big scene, not with an accumulation of little scenes. His characters do not speak in the cut and thrust of actual dialogue; rather, they have arias, formal set-speeches in a formal setting.

The plot works that way, too. In *American Renaissance* F. O. Matthiessen says of *The Scarlet Letter* that "its symmetrical design is built around the three scenes on the scaffold of the pillory." True enough: there is a scene at the beginning, in the middle, and at the end; the three scaffold scenes rise up as the actual scaffold of the plot, giving it symmetry and formal poise. But that is something we recognize retrospectively; it is impossible for someone reading the book for the first time to say after reading the first two appearances on the pillory, "Two down, one to go."

Of equal structural importance is the way Hawthorne leads us to expect a private meeting between Hester and Dimmesdale. A discussion solely of the scaffold scenes in the novel's structure cannot account for our sense that the retreat into the forest is, as Hawthorne tells us it is, "the point whither their pathway had so long been tending." Since the novel centers on what happened when Hester and Dimmesdale were together privately, it builds a necessity for them to meet privately again, to meet and take up together what they had lived with separately. There is a prolonged postponement of this inevitable confrontation.

It is accurate to say that the three scaffold scenes are exactly half of the novel's design. The scaffold marks the necessity for public recognition, a place where that recognition must sooner or later be made. The other half of the picture is the forest where the private recognition must be made. Glade and pillory, these are the two ends of the road down which the novel moves.

A helpful question here is: where does the following sentence occur in the novel—near the beginning, the middle, or the end? Hawthorne writes that the face of Hester Prynne "was like a mask; or, rather, like the frozen calmness of a dead woman's features; owing this dreary resemblance to the fact that Hester was actually dead, in respect to any claim of sympathy." The answer to this question may tell us a good deal about the way the plot of *The Scarlet Letter* operates.

The sentence could come, of course, at the very beginning of the book when Hester is forced to stand alone facing the townspeople, when they point out to her that she is "actually dead" so far as their capacity to treat her as a woman instead of a "type of sin" is concerned. The sentence could also come in the middle section of the book when Hawthorne is describing the daily terms of Hester's new life, when on her errands through the city to the darkened sick rooms she must drop her eyes and assume a coldness of expression so that she will not have to endure the townspeople staring at her letter.

But the sentence describing Hester's aspect comes in chapter XXI, "The New England Holiday." Coming there, near the bitter end, it shows us that Hawthorne's descriptions remain, in one very important sense, static. Over and over again Hawthorne repeats the same device or provides a different context for the same meaning. There is a continual alternation between demands for speech ("Speak out the name!") and demands for silence ("Hush, hush.") Repeatedly Hester hushes Pearl when Pearl pesters her mother about who made her or cries for a rose. When Hester says to Dimmesdale that what they did "had a consecration of its own," Dimmesdale replies, "Hush, Hester." When at the end she asks him what he seeks in eternity, Dimmesdale again sighs, "Hush, Hester, hush." With the hushing there is also a pattern of great, startling sounds. Dimmesdale screams at midnight and hears his voice echoing about the hills; Pearl's shriek at the brookside "reverberated on all sides." The sighing wind in the forest, the far-off sound of Dimmesdale's voice, which Hester hears from her position outside the church, and, most dramatically, Pearl's continual laughing indicate the great auditory resonance of the book. In "Ethan Brand" Hawthorne wrote that "Laughter, when out of place, mistimed, or bursting forth from a disordered state of feeling, may be the most terrible modulation of the human voice." It was so in "My Kinsman, Major Molineux"; it is so in *The Scarlet Letter.* While Hawthorne works extremely hard to elaborate the A—even flashing it across the cope of Heaven—there are far more convincing and successful reverberations in the laughter of Pearl at what are, for her parents, all the wrong places.

The central sin of the book, adultery, is a close analogue to Original Sin; Hester gives Dimmesdale the apple of sexual knowledge; they are forced out of Paradise (the soul-saving, repressive paradise that Boston, the City of Man, represents). The plot tells, in one sense, the story of exile; there are, throughout the book, many journeys. Hester walks from prison to scaffold, and later through the streets; Chillingworth plods around the forest looking for medicinal herbs; Dimmesdale, near the end, wanders from the forest to the town. The book emphasizes these casual and formal motions—"A Forest Walk" and "The Procession"—to show how paths meet and cross in public and in private. In *The Scarlet Letter* the minds of the central figures fall in and out of their "accustomed tracks."

Hester pays in public and expiates her sin in private; Dimmesdale pays in private and expiates his sin in public. Evil is emblazoned on Hester, and she keeps her sanity; Dimmesdale loses his sanity by keeping his evil a secret. At the opening of the novel the people stand in rigid censure, motionless; at the end, there is a pageant of Indians and sailors, and Pearl spinning through them. In this counterpoise the narrative power accumulates through a series of static scenes separated by long stretches of time. That power does not fully gather itself and burst into action until the entire story veers off into another direction, when the two stories—Hester–Pearl and Dimmesdale–Chillingworth—come together. The first half of the novel oscillates between the two histories. On the one hand we see Hester and Pearl, enduring together the stings of the community. The emphasis is on Hester's life; the few encounters between her and the others suggest her loneliness. When she meets Dimmesdale she meets him in public (Governor Bellingham's manse) where she must operate on his ability to apprehend what she is saying as something radically more than what her public voice indicates: "Thou wast my pastor, and hadst charge of my soul, and knowest me better than these men can." But Dimmesdale did not only beget Pearl; he begot Chillingworth as well; thus, the first half of the novel is also the story of the two men and how they live together.

Compare a chapter in the first half, "The Interview," with one in the second half, "A Flood of Sunshine." They belong to different fictive planes. The first is a scene of temptation; Hester wonders if Chillingworth is "The Black Man." It is an encounter which sets the work in motion; it is done in the rhetoric of formal speech. But "A Flood of Sunshine" shows Hawthorne's attempt to escape the formal emblematic picture and to attain the condition of fiction as a realistic portrayal of the psychological play of two characters. The first half of the book, in which "The Interview" occurs, covers seven years. The second half deals with time in measured hours, just a few days. Between the first and the second scaffold scenes Hawthorne goes over the elapsed time once in terms of Hester and Pearl, then again in terms of Dimmesdale and Chillingworth. Between the second and third scaffold scenes the narrative moves straight ahead, no backtracking.

The difference between the time of the first and second halves of the book lies not solely in the length of the elapsed time but rather in the conception of the way time itself operates. In the first section time is all there for Hawthorne; it exists as a stable and completed unit to be taken up, deployed, shifted, and manipulated. The people are as they are; they are presented in significant, emblematic moments. But in the later chapters, time carries people with it. The characters do not exist in extratemporal moments when Hawthorne can lift them off the continuous screen of time. Time rushes on; there is no time to go back over. People exist not just as they are but as they are becoming.

Now we are better prepared to come to terms with a central question: does *The Scarlet Letter* move toward the forest scene in chapters XVII, XVIII, and IXX or toward the final scaffold scene in chapter XXIII? The book leads us to expect that Hester and Dimmesdale will meet in private before the story is done. Hawthorne gives us, as a place of privacy where antisocial meetings are consummated, the forest. It is the domain of Mistress Hibbins, the "dark recess" from community control. The forest is the amphitheater of the "wild rose-bush." It is the place where the outsider knows "that the deep heart of Nature could pity and be kind to him." In the first chapter Hawthorne plucks a flower from his rose bush and presents it to the reader. "It may serve," he says, "to symbolize some sweet moral blossom, that may be found along the track, or relieve the darkening close of a tale of human frailty and sorrow." In the forest scene he offers the blossom again, in all its vitality, to relieve the darkening tale.

Hester, who has repeatedly been identified as a wanderer of "desert places," meets Dimmesdale, literally, on her own ground. We know they cannot meet in town. Hawthorne makes it impossible for them to meet there. "Hester never thought of meeting him in any narrower privacy than beneath the open sky." It is a personal transaction. As Hester later explains to Pearl, "We must not always talk in the market-place of what happens to us in the forest." "Kisses," she explains, "are not to be given in the market-place."

The tie between Hester and Dimmesdale "like all other ties . . . brought along with it its obligation." "Having cast off all duty towards other human beings, there remained a duty towards him." Hester recognizes human responsibility as a primitive social contract, the most primitive possible. She thinks of herself as "playing a part," a social role in the world. But with Dimmesdale, she feels that the part is generated entirely from within, not stamped upon her by public power.

In preparation for the meeting Hawthorne gives us two chapters dealing with Hester and Pearl together, domestic scenes, which develop a familiar intimacy. Dimmesdale in his nocturnal vigils before his looking glass, has asked the same question Hester has in her lonely walks through the city streets and out in the wilderness—Who am I? Am I the being I privately know myself to be, or am I the person this formidable community insists on my being? Why is secrecy and shame the reward for engaging my deepest energy?

The most dramatic scene in the book answers these questions with imaginative generosity. This scene has always seemed to me—in spite of the usual attention paid to the three great pillory scenes—the finest thing in the novel and its true center. One day, by chance Arthur Dimmesdale and Hester Prynne meet on the outskirts of town. They talk only a bit, but their conversation manages to release all their original passion. The first question when the adulterers meet is about each other's "bodily existence." This far apart they have come. They had been "intimately connected in their former life, but now stood coldly shuddering." After all the proliferation of meaning, "The soul beheld its features in the mirror of the passing moment." It is, for me, the most beautiful sentence Hawthorne ever wrote. The entire book has raised the question: how and where does a soul behold its features? No speeches. "Without a word more spoken" the two of them in a dream-like state "glided back into the shadow of the woods." The richness of the prose indicates that what is occurring is a re-efflorescence of their original sin; they respond to each other as private persons rather than as official personages and "now felt themselves, at least, inhabitants of the same sphere."

"When they found a voice to speak, it was, at first, only to utter remarks and inquiries such as any two acquaintances might have made, about the gloomy sky, the threatening storm . . ." We wait and wait and what happens? Very simply, Hester Prynne and Arthur Dimmesdale talk about the weather. Which is entirely right: we see the characters meeting each other with the customary social awkwardness. The great jar of the scene is that suddenly, in the midst of categorical punishment and the proliferation of symbolic significance, two sinners emerge from behind their social disguises to expose their humanity.

In "The Pastor and His Parishioner," the roles are reversed; Hester gives her pastoral counsel and takes off her cap; the whole scene vibrates with her released sexuality. "Her sex, her youth, and the whole richness of her beauty, came back from what men call the irrevocable past, and clustered themselves, with her maiden hope, and happiness before unknown, within the magic circle of this hour."

Holmes said of Hawthorne that "talking with him was almost like love-making." In the forest scene of *The Scarlet Letter,* talking becomes a kind of love-making. Since this is the only scene where the lovers privately come together, their long separation produces extreme richness of feeling in the smallest word.

"Alone, Hester!"

"Thou shalt not go alone!" answered she, in a deep whisper.

Then all was spoken.

The tongue of flame is resonant silence. It is Hawthorne's moment of terrible simplicity—the novel, the huge super-structure of multiplying allegorical signs splinters down to all that needs, for the time, to be said—all that, for this time, can be said. It is an arresting declaration; the form of the great work almost seems to catch its breath, for its central point has just been laid bare in small words. Hawthorne accomplishes in silence what he could not in great sound, for the point of *The Scarlet Letter* is to subvert the resonance of public speech. Hester cries out for forgiveness, admitting that Chillingworth is her husband; when Dimmesdale is staggered, "With sudden and desperate tenderness, she threw her arms around him, and pressed his head against her bosom; little caring though his cheek rested on the scarlet letter." The image is as powerful as anything in our literature. Hester whispers, "What we did had a consecration of its own." That line is justly celebrated as the finest in the book. But what I cherish are the next two short sentences: Hester says, "We felt it so! We said so to each other!"

But the heretical reality of the scene is brief. Hester urges flight to Europe; Dimmesdale knows he can not run away. When I first began teaching *The Scarlet Letter* to Cornell students in the late 1960s, the scene in the forest was what most appealed to them. The imaginative power of the real encounter felt right; that was *their* Hawthorne—the "*real*" Hawthorne—as if the rest of the book was just the time he lived in. When the catchphrases on campus were "Make Love, Not War" and "Flower Power," young readers tended to sentimentalize the book for their own radical and visionary purposes. Now, however, students are more inclined to accept the forest scene for what it is, a "flood of sunshine" that is by definition only momentary. The right reading comes at great cost—sometimes I long for the days when enthusiasm got it wrong. But Hawthorne himself placed his great scene of escape in a stern context of return.

The Scarlet Letter has for its subject the tension between personal desire and community solidarity. In the forest scene we have been presented with the first; now, at the end of the book, the energy released in the forest is poured into the old context, the brutalizing categories of the Puritan state. Dimmesdale achieves what Hawthorne calls "the tongue of flame"; his congregation senses a power and humanity in him that they had never known before. But when he emerges from the church and totters to the pillory, the book begins to falter. In the forest scene Hester had pleaded, "Do anything, save to lie down and die." On the scaffold Dimmesdale lies down and dies. Hawthorne seems to indicate that Dimmesdale has thus saved his immortal soul. The problem is that in throwing himself on God's mercy, Dimmesdale abandons Hester and Pearl. As Michael Colacurcio puts it: "fleeing from the arms of Hester Prynne to those of the heavenly bridegroom his own (rather too feminine) nature finally manages to prefer." Dimmesdale has never been Hester's husband, Colacurcio insists, "and it would only be a little cruel to suggest that he is dying to evade that very role." D. H. Lawrence puts it aptly: the ending shows Dimmesdale "dodging into death, leaving Hester dished."

At the end of the book Hawthorn retreats into Phoebe-talk: "The angel and apostle of the coming revelation must be a woman, indeed, but lofty, pure, and beautiful: and wise, moreover not through dusky grief, but the ethereal medium of joy and showing how sacred love should make us happy." Sacvan Bercovitch has it backwards when he writes of these lines that "the entire novel tends toward this moment of reconciliation." Bercovitch says "this is not some formulaic Victorian ending." I think it is: the critical necessity is to see that Hawthorne certainly does mean this, and at the same time to see that it is a violent contradiction of the most serious motive in the novel. We must not mistake the statement at the end of the book for anything other than what it is—a pious retraction.

There is, however, on the very last page, a partial recovery. Dimmesdale has celebrated in his dying sermon the great America to be; what we know of the future is that Hester returns. She knows her fate. In chapter 14 she had protested that "it lies not in the pleasure of the magistrates to take off this badge." She returns to bear that out. Finally the A is Hester and Hester knows it. "There was more real life for Hester Prynne, here in New England than in that unknown region where Pearl had found a home." The A becomes her. Hester belongs in Boston precisely because she is the single person who has not been allowed to belong there. She has turned a badge of shame into a coat of arms.

Chapter Six

Emerson, Blithedale, *and* The Bostonians

Every time I teach my "New England Renaissance" course I ask my students, Who was Ralph Waldo Emerson? Year by year the students' answers get vaguer (although I remind myself that on this very campus over forty years ago Stephen Whicher made the same complaint). Today's students aren't sure when Emerson lived, and they seem surprised that he was just a year older than Hawthorne. They usually can't respond to my invitation to name anything Emerson wrote. F. O. Matthiessen rightly claimed "The sentence was his unit," so I present to the class a handout of ten of my own favorite Emerson "sentences," and we spend an hour locating them, exploring their meaning and contexts:

1. Crossing a bare common in snow puddles, at twilight, under a clouded sky, without having in my thoughts any occurrence of special good fortune, I have enjoyed a perfect exhilaration. I am glad to the brink of fear.
2. Hitch your wagon to a star.
3. A foolish consistency is the hobgoblin of little minds.
4. By the rude bridge that arched the flood,
    Their flag to April's breeze unfurled,
   Here once the embattled farmers stood
    And fired the shot heard round the world.

5. I dreamed that I floated at will in the great Ether, and I saw this world floating also not far off, but diminished to the size of an apple. Then an angel took it in his hand & brought it to me and said, "This must thou eat." And I ate the world.

6.   The eager fate which carried thee
       Took the largest part of me:
       For this losing is true dying;
       This is lordly man's down-lying,
       This his slow but sure reclining,
       Star by star his world resigning.

7. I am God in nature; I am a weed by the wall.

8. I greet you at the beginning of a great career.

9.   Eve softly with her womb
       Bit him to death

10. (On the Fugitive Slave Law) And this filthy enactment was made in the nineteenth century, by people who could read and write. I will not obey it, by God.

My students recognize one or two of these, usually slightly garbled versions of 3 or 4. While doing this exercise, I finally clarified something I had puzzled over for years. In Emerson's search for "*A national man*" (his italics) he wrote that John Brown's speech at Charlestown and Lincoln's Gettysburg Address were "the two best specimens of eloquence we have had in this country." When Brown was hanged, Emerson wrote that the abolitionist's death "would make the gallows as glorious as the Cross." Hawthorne's verdict in 1862 was that "No man was ever more justly hanged." Hawthorne remembered Emerson's verdict almost as I had remembered it—substituting "venerable" for "glorious." What Emerson actually wrote was that the hanging of John Brown "will make the gallows glorious *like* the cross," not "*as* glorious *as*" (and Emerson omitted the sentence completely when the lecture was included in his book *Society and Solitude*). Hawthorne had heard the slightly incorrect version in England; when he returned home, he said he was glad to hear that Emerson had "put John Brown at a somewhat lower elevation than Jesus Christ."

Misunderstandings aside, however, the most important story about the Emerson and Hawthorne relationship is a constant and lifelong process of each man saying yes and no to the other. I doubt that one legend is true—it is too good to be true—that when Emerson wrote *Nature* in the Old Manse he situated his desk so that he could look out the window, whereas when Hawthorne wrote his dark stories at the same desk he turned it around to face the wall. What we do know is true is the preface to *Mosses from an Old Manse,* where Hawthorne pays tribute to Emerson sitting in this room at this desk, where he "used to watch the Assyrian dawn and the Paphian sunset," a phrase from *Nature;* Hawthorne speaks of Emerson's "intellectual fire, as a beacon burning on a hill-top" (only to provide immediately a satiric portrait of Emerson's disciples, "a variety of queer, strangely dressed, oddly behaved mortals, most of whom took upon themselves to be important agents of the world's destiny, yet were simply bores of a very intense water"). The eminent Emersonian Joel Porte has suggested to me that the entire preface to *Mosses from an Old Manse* should be considered as Hawthorne's sustained argument with Emerson.

In other places, though, Hawthorne can sound exactly like Emerson. Holgrave, in *The House of Seven Gables* cries out, " 'Shall we never, never get rid of this past? It lies upon the Present like a giant's dead body!' " Holgrave seems to have been immersed in "The American Scholar" or "The Divinity School Address" when he complains,

> "A dead man sits on all our judgment seats; and living judges do but search out and repeat his decisions. We read in dead men's books! We laugh at dead men's jokes, and cry at dead men's pathos! We are sick of dead men's diseases, physical and moral, and die of the same remedies with which dead doctors killed their patients! We worship the living Deity according to dead men's forms and creeds. Whatever we seek to do, of our own free motion, a dead man's icy hand obstructs us!"

This is pure Emerson—in its substance, in its diction, and in its hortatory rhythms.

But again there is a sardonic negative to the oratorical positive. In "The Celestial Railroad" Hawthorne has fun with a cavern at the end of a valley where in olden times "dwelt two cruel giants, Pope and Pagan" (from *Pilgrim's Progress*); nowadays "these vile old troglodytes are no longer there" because "another terrible giant has thrust himself" into their

place: "He is German by birth, and is called 'Giant Transcendentalist.' "
He looks "like a heap of fog and duskiness. He shouted after us, but in so
strange a phraseology that we knew not what he meant, nor whither to be
encouraged or affrighted."

Nathaniel Hawthorne and Ralph Waldo Emerson—the two enemies,
the two opponents, the two friends—constantly *go* at each other, in their
leisurely walks, their years of Concord conversations, their outpourings of
books. It was natural, as Henry James said in *Hawthorne,* that "Emerson, as
a sort of spiritual sun-worshipper, could have attached but a moderate
value to Hawthorne's cat-like faculty of seeing in the dark." How could
Hawthorne be on intimate terms with a man who, while still in his teens,
had proclaimed their shared era as "the age of the first person singular"
and later described himself as "a seeker with no Past at his back"? No Past
at your back? Hawthorne had the Past not only at his back but everywhere he turned.

In at least one regard they are twin branches on the same tree. Emerson
says that "the use of the outer creation is to give us language for the beings
and changes of the inward creation." When he proclaims that "particular
natural facts are symbols of particular spiritual facts" his words are close to
Hawthorne's allegorical method; when "we are symbols and inhabit symbols," we find ourselves in the epistemological and aesthetic realm staked
out in my previous chapter on the symbolic texture of *The Scarlet Letter.*
Going a giant step further in this regard, the gifted scholar David Van Leer
has noticed that in *Nature* Emerson's assertion that man is uplifted "into
infinite space" is echoed exactly when in the forest scene of *The Scarlet
Letter* Hester casts her shameful badge "into infinite space." Emerson says
his idealism "leaves me in the splendid labyrinth of my perceptions, to
wander without end." Hester is left "to wander without a clew in the dark
labyrinth of mind." "Infinite space," "wander," "labyrinth."

Moreover, compare Emerson's "Do not believe the past" with Hester's
passionate cry, "The past is gone!" Emerson wrote in *Nature:* "At the gates
of the forest, the surprised man of the world is forced to leave his city es-
timates of great and small, wise and foolish. The knapsack of custom falls
off his back with the first step he takes into these precincts. Here is sanctity
which shames our religions. The incommunicable trees begin to persuade
us to live with them, and to quit our life of solemn trifles. Here no history,

or church, or state is interpolated on the divine sky." In *The Scarlet Letter*
Hester "never thought of meeting Dimmesdale in any narrower privacy
than beneath the open sky." From her bosom Hester takes off the scarlet
letter; "the knapsack of custom falls off" Emerson's back. "The sanctity
which shames our religions" becomes "a consecration of its own." Even
Emerson's "incommunicable trees" become, in Hawthorne's pathetic fal-
lacy, emotionally articulate: "one solemn old tree groaned dolefully to another, as if telling the sad story of the pair that sat beneath."

Emerson has usually been culturally placed at the head of "The Party
of Hope," and Hawthorne has been numbered with "The Party of
Doubt." What I have been trying to outline with the above examples is
that the kinship is much closer and their agonized conversations much
richer. After one long evening of such conversation—to which Hawthorne listened without contributing—Emerson remarked, "Hawthorne
rides well his horse of the night." And in his journal, the day after Hawthorne's funeral, Emerson wrote, "It would have been a happiness, doubtless to both of us, to have come into habits of unreserved intercourse. It
was easy to talk with him,—there were no barriers,—only, he said so
little, that I talked too much."

In *The Blithedale Romance,* Miles Coverdale says that during a brief period
of confinement, he "read interminably in Mr. Emerson's Essays" (note
the adverb). A little later he asks Priscilla, "did you ever see Miss Margaret
Fuller?" and says, "this very letter is from her." Surely Hawthorne is per-
forming a little sleight-of-hand trick of misdirection when Coverdale
says, "you reminded me of her." How could the anemic Priscilla remind
anyone of Margaret Fuller? The frail girl doesn't look, think, or talk like
her. Zenobia, though, clearly thinks and talks like Margaret Fuller. One
modern critic, Darrel Abel, describes Ms. Fuller as "a homely girl, dumpy,
long-necked, and near-sighted, with a strident nasal voice and distracting
mannerisms. From her awareness that she was physically repellent she de-
cided to be 'bright and ugly.'" Emerson charitably said, "Her features
were disagreeable to most persons so long as they were little acquainted
with her, that is, until the features were dissolved in the power of the expression." She was full of "great tenderness and sympathy." Looking over

her papers he concluded that "the unlooked for trait in all these journals to me is the Woman, poor woman; they are all hysterical. She is bewailing her virginity and languishing for a husband."

But, as Alcott said, Margaret Fuller was "the most brilliant talker of the day." James said she was "*the* talker; she was the genius of talk." In conversation her self-infatuation was grandiose: "I now know all the people worth knowing in America, and I find no intellect comparable to my own." Emerson noted that, indeed, "Margaret occasionally lets slip some phrase betraying the presence of a rather mountainous ME." Often her egotism seems like a pathological version of Emerson's doctrine of compensation: "I hate not to be beautiful. I am not fitted to be loved. No one loves me. I have no child, and the woman in me has so craved this experience. The Woman in me kneels and weeps in tender rapture; the Man in me rushes forth, only to be baffled. Yet the time will come, when, from the union of this tragic king and queen, shall be born a radiant sovereign self." No wonder Hawthorne jotted in his notebook, in 1841, "I was invited to dine at Mr. Bancroft's yesterday, with Miss Margaret Fuller; but Providence had given me some business to do; for which I was very thankful!"

Their acquaintance was what one would expect. James concluded that the relationship was doomed from the start, given the temperament of both; Margaret "in whose intellect high noon seemed ever to reign, as twilight did in Hawthorne's own." But, James adds, Margaret Fuller was "the only literary lady of eminence whom there is any sign of Hawthorne's having known; she was proud, passionate, and eloquent," and she provided him with a model for "the beautiful and sumptuous Zenobia, a woman in all the force of the term." The resemblance is all but uncanny in some regards, and perhaps most importantly in this: Margaret Fuller remarks sadly that "These gentlemen are surprised that I write no better, because I talk so well. But I have served a long apprenticeship to the one, none to the other. I shall write better, but never, I think, so well as I talk; for then I feel inspired. My voice excites me, my pen, never." Compare this to Zenobia's outburst: "The pen is not for woman. Her power is too natural and immediate. It is with the living voice alone that she can compel the world to recognize the light of her intellect and the depth of her heart." Coverdale ruefully concludes that Zenobia's "poor little stories and tracts never half did justice to her intellect." No, she had a "mind full of weeds" and should be "a stump oratress," or perhaps "the stage would have been her proper sphere."

Margaret Fuller—Sarah Margaret Fuller Ossoli—late in her life, in Rome, proclaimed, "I love best to be a woman; but womanhood is at present too straitly bounded to give me scope. Once I was almost all intellect; now I am almost all feeling. Nature vindicates her rights, and I feel all Italy glowing beneath the Saxon crust." Emerson described Margaret as "an exotic in New England, a foreigner from some more sultry and expansive clime." Looking back to William Ware's *Zenobia,* a best seller of 1838, Hawthorne said he wanted to call his Brook Farm novel *Zenobia,* "but Mr. Ware has anticipated me in that."

What Hawthorne did when he turned the real woman into a fictional heroine was to give her an extraordinary physical beauty to equal her intellectual brilliance. Coverdale says to himself that Zenobia is "a woman to whom wedlock had thrown wide the gates of mystery"; repeatedly he tries to stop thinking about it, but there obsessively comes "pertinaciously the thought, 'Zenobia is a wife; Zenobia has lived and loved! There is no folded petal, no latent dewdrop, in this perfectly developed rose!' " In language that prefigures his response to the great lady at the Lord Mayor's dinner in Liverpool (which I quoted earlier, "I never should have thought of touching her"), Hawthorne has Coverdale say, "I should not, under any circumstances, have fallen in love with Zenobia," although (or because?) "the whole woman was alive with a passionate intensity" and "any passion would have become her well; and passionate love, perhaps, the best of all." The entire relationship is a kind of luxurious prurience: when Zenobia, "shivering playfully," announces that "as for the garb of Eden, I shall not assume it till after May-day!" Coverdale goes into a little swoon, mumbling that "Assuredly, Zenobia could not have intended it,—the fault must have been entirely in my imagination." He can't stop visualizing "a picture of that fine, perfectly developed figure in Eve's earliest garment"—or, rather, before Sophia asked her husband to take it out, Coverdale had said, "I almost fancied myself actually beholding it." Coverdale rhapsodizes that "We seldom meet with women nowadays, and in this country, who impress us as being women at all,—their sex fades away, and goes for nothing, in ordinary intercourse. Not so with Zenobia.

One felt an influence breathing out of her such as we might suppose to come from Eve, when she was just made, and her Creator brought her to Adam, saying 'Behold! here is woman!' " Poor Coverdale—he has to admit, after glimpsing Zenobia's naked shoulder beneath her neckerchief—that "It struck me as a great piece of good fortune that there should be just that glimpse."

In 1850 *The Scarlet Letter* was published in Boston and the National Women's Rights convention was held in Worcester. It is an appealing coincidence to consider. I have argued that *The Scarlet Letter* is in one sense a great historical novel, in its recapturing of seventeenth-century New England. The book is also very much about nineteenth-century America. It is a portrait of the Puritan past, the first great American community; it is also a testament to the immediate circumstances around its date of composition, reflecting a contemporaneous and deeply felt anxiety about the place of Woman—about marriage, divorce, birth control, suffrage, and woman's place in the social economy of 1850. In *Disorderly Conduct, Visions of Gender in Victorian America,* Carroll Smith-Rosenberg provides instructive stories of the women's rights movement of the 1830s, 1840s, and 1850s. Their causes included freeing women from their subservient role in the family, and thereby freeing them from male domination. Sarah Grimké challenged women to read and interpret the Bible for themselves; Grimké fought against the "Go home and spin advice of the domestic tyrant. Women should rise from the degradation and bondage to which we have been consigned by man." And in this context Adultery in *The Scarlet Letter* represents a cultural anxiety about where and to whom a woman "belongs." David B. Davis has convincingly argued that "the literary ideal of feminine perfection has become inflated to a point beyond even the dream of realization. At the same time, a changing economy undermined the sources of masculine authority in the home. It is significant that popular writers expressed their fear of change in specifically sexual terms. A husband's loss of prestige and power could best be symbolized in the outrage of sexual dishonor. Social disorganization could be represented in its ultimate form in the union of sex and death."

In his final sentence Davis makes the same adjustment we need to make when we turn from the tragic career of Hester Prynne to the pathetic death of Zenobia Moody. Here, too, Hawthorne clearly has Margaret Fuller in mind. When she drowned in a shipwreck just off Fire Island in the summer of 1850, Emerson recorded in his journal, "I have lost in her my audience"; he sent Thoreau to the scene to find and recover, if possible, Margaret's effects. Hawthorne seems to have known a good deal about the tragedy (from it he got the name for *Blithedale's* spooky villain—one of the victims of the disaster was a Henry Westervelt). Hawthorne had it much on his mind, a year later, when he described Zenobia's death by drowning.

He also had a source closer to home, something in his own *Notebooks*—ten paragraphs about his participation in the recovery of the body of a young woman, Martha Hunt, who drowned herself in a local river. The midnight search is so graphic and painful that Sophia omitted the account from her edition of her husband's notebooks; the full story was not published until their son Julian's *Hawthorne and His Wife* (1885). In an *Atlantic* book review Thomas Wentworth Higginson said that the account was "almost too frightful to put into words,—certainly to be put into type," and complained that had Julian "introduced a series of photographs from the Paris morgue, the result would not have been more horrible."

When Hawthorne used those notebook passages in *Blithedale* he kept an oddly touching detail about the woman's lost shoe, changed some things for symbolic importance—the wound in the real girl's eye was shifted to Zenobia's heart—and he refrained from the actual grisly aspects such as the copious bleeding and the anticipated gross swelling of the corpse. Ellery Channing's rake becomes old Silas Foster's pole. But the essentials remain: in the notebook entry Hawthorne wrote that the body's rigidity was dreadful to behold," and in *Blithedale* Coverdale wails, "Ah, that rigidity!" In the notebook the girl "was the very image of a death-agony," and in the novel Zenobia is "the marble image of death agony." Notebook: "Her arms had stiffened in the act of struggling; and were bent before her, with hands clenched." Novel: "Her arms had grown rigid in the act of struggling, and were bent before her with clenched hands."

Entirely new, however, is Coverdale's morbid censure: "Zenobia, I have often thought, was not quite simple in her death. She had seen pictures, I suppose, of drowned persons in lithe and graceful attitudes." Coverdale cruelly asks, "Has not the world come to an awfully sophisticated pass, when we cannot even put ourselves to death in whole-hearted simplicity?" Hawthorne spares us the grim details, but the fictional drowning is even more horrible than the actual one—the novelistic one resonates with a grotesque sense of punishment as well as naked tragedy.

In 1879 Henry James said that "the finest thing in *The Blithedale Romance* is the character of Zenobia." She is "the nearest approach that Hawthorne has made to the complete creation of a *person*." Comparing her to other versions of Hawthorne's dark ladies, James declares that Zenobia is "a more definite image, produced by a great multiplicity of touches." This verdict seems to me both true and false. If we look ahead to Miriam in *The Marble Faun* we find a woman with "a great deal of color in her nature," "a beautiful woman," with "dark eyes and black, abundant hair," "a dark glory." She belongs, that is, with Hester and Beatrice and Zenobia; they are all essentially one woman; all their characteristics are interchangeable, and the sameness suggests an obsession in Hawthorne with the very opposite of the Dove Lady he officially pays homage to in the figures of Priscilla and Phoebe and Hilda. The Dark Lady lives—lives variously, frankly, openly, sexually. She is a welcoming attitude to experience. She takes life as it comes, and does not transmute it or "spiritualize" it into acceptably polite domesticity.

In my analysis of *The Scarlet Letter* I cited some instances of what I called "cross-cultural references." We find them at work in *Blithedale,* too: for example, the ominous Westervelt describes Priscilla as

one of those delicate, nervous young creatures, not uncommon in New England, and whom I suppose to have become what we find them by the gradual refining away of the physical system among your women. Some philosophers choose to glorify this habit of body by terming it spiritual; but, in my opinion, it is rather the effect of unwholesome food, bad air, lack of out-door exercise, and neglect of bathing, on the part of these damsels and their female progenitors, all resulting in a kind of hereditary dyspepsia. Zenobia, even with her uncomfortable surplus of vitality, is far the better model of womanhood.

Hawthorne, at least officially, is one of those "philosophers," but he also wrote Westervelt's powerful speech, and he created Zenobias throughout his work, on one hand glorifying the "spiritual" and on the other glorifying the "uncomfortable surplus of vitality."

In chapter XIII of *The Scarlet Letter,* "Another View of Hester," we are told that "The world's law was no law for her mind." She is a revolutionary, a woman who joins forces with "men of the sword" who "had overthrown nobles and kings" and who espoused a radical "sphere of theory" that had "rearranged the whole system of ancient prejudice." "Hester Prynne imbibed this spirit. She assumed a freedom of speculation which our forefathers, had they known of it,, would have held to be a deadlier crime than that stigmatized by the scarlet letter." Indeed, "she might, and not improbably would, have suffered death from the stern tribunals of the period, for attempting to undermine the foundations of the Puritan establishment. A dark question often rose into her mind, with reference to the whole race of womanhood."

In *Blithedale* Zenobia echoes Hester's thoughts, declaiming "with great earnestness and passion, nothing short of anger, on the injustices which the world did to women, and equally to itself, by not allowing them, in freedom and honor, and with the fullest welcome, their natural utterance in public." Zenobia expresses nothing but disdain for Priscilla as "the type of womanhood such as man has spent centuries in making it." Ironically (or, one might say, altogether naturally and logically), it is precisely that feeble "type of womanhood" who wins Hollingsworth's love; he blusters on about woman as "the most admirable handiwork of God, in her true place and character." This brute, a "tolerably educated bear," is the mouthpiece for all the old chauvinist clichés: Woman's "place is at man's side. Her office, that of sympathizer; the unreserved, unquestioning believer." If she tries anything else, "I would call upon my own sex to use its physical force." Hollingsworth is misogyny incarnate. That is exactly the problem. He is too easy; there is no rigor to his thought, nothing majestic in his words or deeds. When she loses him, Zenobia loses a stereotype.

The real achievement of *Blithedale,* as James emphasized in 1879, is Coverdale's response to Zenobia; it is meaningful cultural criticism insofar as the central relationship portrays the response of a reserved New England gentleman to an exotic woman:

> "Mr. Coverdale," she said one day, as she saw me watching her, while she arranged my gruel on the table, "I have been exposed to a great deal of eye-shot in the few years of my mixing in the world, but never, I think, to precisely such glances as you are in the habit of favoring me with. I seem to interest you very much; and yet—or else a woman's instinct is for once deceived—I cannot reckon you as an admirer. What are you seeking to discover in me?"
>
> "The mystery of your life," answered I, surprised into truth by the unexpectedness of her attack.

Here is the vital and demanding *Blithedale:* Coverdale peering at the dark lady. That is, the tension Hawthorne has made is that between the shy, distrustful New England masculine ego and the feminine incarnation of everything that challenges and threatens to destroy the world in which that ego operates.

Throughout *Blithedale* we learn that Zenobia is a kind of witch: "her gruel was very wretched stuff, with almost invariably the smell of pine smoke upon it, like the evil taste that is said to mix itself up with a witch's best concocted dainties." To Zenobia Hollingsworth says that Coverdale "talks about your being a witch." Coverdale speaks of "Zenobia, the sorceress herself" who is "fair enough to tempt Satan with a force reciprocal to his own." Witchcraft, in *The Scarlet Letter* and *The Blithedale Romance,* is a symbol of forbidden knowledge. In many places in *The Scarlet Letter,* witchery is explicitly linked to sexual abandon. Hawthorne's fascination with the metaphor of witchcraft for sexuality is an indication of how intensely he understood the Puritan categories; for the Puritans, witchcraft expressed a religion of demonic power. It was a rival to the true New England faith, Puritan Christianity turned into a nightmare of physical potions and sensual rites. Witchcraft is the symbol of the sexual night; it celebrates in the forest all that is denied in Boston, the citadel of repressive community power.

Here we begin to understand why Hester Prynne is more successful than Zenobia in focusing and controlling the novel in which she appears. *Blithedale* operates in a kind of social vacuum; the community does not bind its agents. Zenobia is not so much the artistic center of the book as she is the center of our attention in a book that now and again falters; Hawthorne does not seem to know how to develop the progression of events to indicate what is at once so fascinating and so reprehensible in his heroine. Miles Coverdale, who has given himself away at a dozen different places in the narrative as a man in love with Zenobia, gasps out his confession in the last line: "I—I—myself—was in love—with—Priscilla!" If the last word of the sentence were "Zenobia"—not "Priscilla"— Coverdale's stammering admission would be clearer: the woman who excites him (and to whom he would wait until the last word to pay explicit tribute) is the exotic feminist, not the pallid seamstress. But when Coverdale says that Priscilla is the object of his chilly heart, it is difficult to know how we are to measure out his collapse. Since Hawthorne gave all the honors to a Phoebe in the novel preceding *Blithedale,* and paid tribute to another dove lady in the novel that follows, the question is not only Coverdale's perception but also Hawthorne's.

With the figure of Hester Prynne he was able to maintain clarity. His sense of Puritan society was the counterforce necessary for him to make meaning out of the war between what James called "his evasive and inquisitive tendencies." Hester is a high-spirited woman who is repressed by the masculine Boston world. She shows how, in that society, the primitive impulse constantly engaged in eruptive combat with public law, how the primitive powers of the unconscious fought the censor of society. Hester expresses a drastic and convincing mutiny because she says, in effect, "I am a citizen of somewhere else" and implores Dimmesdale to make passage with her into that realm. Outwardly a model of submission and obedience, Hester in her soul says No in thunder to the restraints of civilization. What makes the book both coherent and powerful is that Hester's defiance meets an equal, opposite force in the Puritan community. When Hawthorne creates the vital Zenobia in *Blithedale* he makes a force opposite to her but nowhere near commensurate in imaginative power. Hester is almost rubbed out behind the A; Zenobia shows up Blithedale for what it is, a shallow Utopia. (Margaret Fuller herself said that when she visited Brook Farm she found herself "in the amusing position of a conservative" and she expressed no dismay when the brief experiment failed.) We can understand how Hester's fate is tragic, but Zenobia seems to be the victim of that shy, furtive half of Coverdale's nature and also of Hawthorne's ingrained conservatism. In *The Scarlet Letter* Hawthorne rendered with sufficient density the force of the community that opposed Hester, a force that made her struggle the very texture of the book. Puritan society was the bracing restriction which Hawthorne needed to be at his best. In the Puritan allegorical sharpness and explicitness, the quest for reality, the quest for meaning, became a part of the quest for social and individual identity. Imaginatively, it is a long way from the dark streets of Boston to the "counterfeit" Arcadia where Hawthorne spent his time "milking transcendental heifers and pitching Utopian hay." In ceasing to tread the native soil of that part of the American past to which he felt closest, Hawthorne lost his sense of restrictive place, his great sense of the way the community closes in.

Henry James, in *Partial Portraits:*

> There were certain chords in Emerson that did not vibrate at all. I well remember my impression of this on walking with him in the autumn of 1872 through the galleries of the Louvre and, later that winter, through those of the Vatican: his perception of the objects contained in these collections was of the most general order. I was struck with the anomaly of a man so refined and intelligent being so little spoken to by works of art. Hawthorne was for years our author's neighbour at Concord and a little—a very little we gather—his companion. Emerson was unable to read his novels—he thought them "not worthy of him." This is a judgment odd almost to fascination. How strange that he should not have been eager to read almost anything that such a gifted being might have let fall! It was a rare accident that made them live almost side by side so long in the same small New England town, such a fruit of a long Puritan stem, yet with such a difference of taste. Hawthorne's vision was all for the evil and sin of the world; a side of life as to which Emerson's eyes were thickly bandaged.

In *Hawthorne* James speaks glowingly—one could say rapturously—about "the admirable and exquisite Emerson." James says Emerson "was the man of genius of the moment; he was the Transcendentalist *par excel-lence.*" He "had a great charm for people living in a society in which in-trospection—thanks to the want of other entertainment—played almost the part of a social resource." James refers specifically to "a certain occa-sion which made a sensation, an era—the delivery of an address to the Divinity School of Harvard University, on a summer evening in 1838."

The first and justly famous sentence of that address is "In this refulgent summer it has been a luxury to draw the breath of life." In the first book I ever encountered that taught me how to *read* Emerson, Jonathan Bishop's *Emerson on the Soul,* the sentence is described as "unusually aure-ate." Bishop says, "the immediate rhetorical motive, evidently enough, is shock: an address to a small group of graduating divinity students is not supposed to begin by an appeal to the sensual man." Bishop notes the weirdness of Ralph Waldo Emerson talking like a "voluptuary." And we should note as well that "luxury" is a red flag, *luxuria* being one of the seven deadly sins. As Porte asserts, Emerson seems to be like Ann Hutchinson before the church elders or Hester Prynne before the towns-people: Emerson challenges his distinguished elders on the faculty to consider formal religion unnecessary because Nature provides its own sacraments, a consecration of its own.

Within a year after *Hawthorne* appeared, James embarks on *The Portrait of a Lady,* and we see the presence of Emerson in it as profoundly as we saw his presence in *The Scarlet Letter.* Leon Edel claims that in *Portrait* James was "seeking answers to the transcendentalism of Concord: his novel is a critique of American 'Self-Reliance.' " Emerson had urged his audience, James wrote, to go outside, to seek Nature in the natural atmo-sphere, to "take a picturesque view of one's internal responsibilities, and to find in the landscape of the soul all sorts of fine sunrise and moonlight effects." There we have Isabel Archer's picturesque conceit: "A visit to the recesses of one's spirit was harmless when one returned from it with a lapful of roses." Early on, Isabel Archer is almost fierce in her determi-nation, in true Emersonian style, not to conform or to compromise "for the sake of being more comfortable." She digs in her heels when it comes to her "personal independence." And James himself, almost a quarter of a century later, in "The Beast in the Jungle," would turn a much sterner light—a ghastly light—upon Emerson's "doctrine of the supremacy of the individual to himself" and his advice that "a man should await his call."

As you can find Emerson everywhere in the work of Nathaniel Hawthorne, you can find him everywhere in the work of Henry James. Actually, you find him all over the place. He is the best example, himself, of what he said a man like himself should be, a powerful presence to the writers and thinkers of his age. Not only to Hawthorne and James, but to Melville, to Whitman, to Emily Dickinson, and of course to Thoreau—where would Thoreau have been without him? Yes, Ralph Waldo Emerson is the representative man.

James's editor said *The Bostonians* was the most unpopular book he had ever published. The trouble began with the first installment in the *Century Magazine.* New England readers found the character of Miss Birdseye an insulting caricature. Miss Birdseye is, of course, Nathaniel Hawthorne's sister-in-law, Elizabeth Peabody (who once, after knocking herself cold by walking straight into a lamppost, explained, "I saw it, but failed to realize it"). In her later years Miss Peabody was known as "the Grandmother of Boston." Perhaps I should not have said "of course" just above. James himself denied it vehemently after receiving a note from his brother William saying that the Peabody–Birdseye figure was "really a pretty bad business." Henry replied,

> I am quite appalled by your note . . . you assault me on the subject of my having painted a "portrait from life" of Miss Peabody! I care not a straw what people in general may say about Miss Birdseye—they can say nothing more idiotic and insulting than they have already said about all my books in which there has been any attempt to represent things or persons in America; but I should be very sorry—in fact deadly sick, or fatally ill—if I thought Miss Peabody *herself* supposed I intended to represent her. I absolutely had no shadow of such an intention. I have not seen Miss P. for twenty years, I never had but the most casual observation of her, I didn't know whether she was alive or dead. I am alarmed by the sentence in your letter—"It is really a pretty bad business." Though subordinate, she is, I think, the best figure in the book; she is treated with respect throughout, and every virtue of heroism and disinterestedness is at-

tributed to her. I find this charge on the subject of Miss Peabody a very cold douche indeed.

One wonders, more than a little, what all the fuss is about. Miss Birdseye has "no more outline than a bundle of hay," but she is as wise as she is dotty, and few scenes in the novel are as lovely as Basil Ransom's little horsecar ride with her, where he is positively flirtatious, and she nails him with a murmur, "That's the way Olive Chancellor told me you talked." She is remarkably undeceived for a person so instinctively and programmatically generous. Her gentle drift into death from old age is genuinely poignant. Ransom's last words to her, "I shall remember you as an example of what women are capable of," are quite misunderstood by Olive Chancellor "as an insolent sarcasm," but by this point Olive hates Ransom with all her bruised and savage heart. He had meant what he said literally; no higher tribute could come from the Mississippian: "he thought poor Miss Birdseye, for all her absence of profile, essentially feminine." She is a great lady. Ransom speaks of the "Grandmother of Boston" as if she were his own.

But James realized, soon after publication, that the novel was "born under an evil star." "It has fallen flat. I hoped much of it, and shall be disappointed—having got no money for it, I hoped for a little glory." The general animus toward it continued in its intensity for so long that Scribner's declined to include it in the New York edition of James's work, which hurt him deeply, and all over again, because he felt that the novel had "never received any sort of justice." "I should have liked to review it for the Edition—it would have come out a much truer and curious thing (it was meant to be curious from the first)." "I should have liked to write that preface." In 1879 Boston had said no to *Hawthorne,* and now it was saying no once more, seven years later, to *The Bostonians.* And why not? James started it, having Basil Ransom shout "The city of Boston be damned!"

But it is an absolutely splendid novel, and, as Irving Howe said, "the masterpiece that Hawthorne's book might have been." It is "a free and happy release of aggressive feeling"; James "finds a distinct pleasure in sweeping down on the intellectual frauds and quacks." It is his funniest book. The characters are unforgettable. Whatever one thinks of Miss Birdseye, or her origins, James has her perfectly:

She was a little old lady, with an enormous head . . . the vast, fair, protu-
berant, candid, ungarnished brow, surmounting a pair of weak, kind,
tired-looking eyes, and ineffectually balanced in the rear by a cap which
had the air of falling backward, and which Miss Birdseye suddenly felt
for while she talked, with unsuccessful irrelevant movements. Her face
looked as if it had been soaked, blurred, and made vague by exposure to
some slow dissolvent. The long practice of philanthropy had not given
accent to her features; it had rubbed out their transitions, their meanings.
The waves of sympathy, of enthusiasm, had wrought upon them in the
same way in which the waves of time finally modify the surface of old
marble busts, gradually washing away their sharpness, their details.

Grandly, "the whole moral history of Boston was reflected in her dis-
placed spectacles" (and this constituted Henry's only concession to
William: "The one definite thing about which I had scruple was some
touch about Miss Birdseye's spectacles—I remembered that Miss
Peabody's were always in the wrong place"; but, he continues, "I didn't
see, really, why I should deprive myself of an effect which is common to
a thousand old people").

Every woman in the novel gets the once-over: Mrs. Farrinder, for example,

was a copious, handsome woman, in whom angularity had been cor-
rected by the air of success; she had a rustling dress (it was evident what
she thought about taste), abundant hair of a glossy blackness, a pair of
folded arms, the expression of which seemed to say that rest, in such a
career as hers, was as sweet as it was brief. Mrs. Farrinder, at almost any
time, had the air of being introduced by a few remarks.

Even the accessory figures on the periphery of the main action get a taste
of it: Mrs. Tarrant, Verena's ineffectual old mother, "found herself completely enrolled in the great irregular army of nostrum-mongers, domi-
ciled in humanitary Bohemia. It absorbed her like a social swamp; she
sank into it a little more every day, without measuring the inches of her
descent. Now she stood there up to her chin; it may probably be said of
her that she had touched bottom." These wicked descriptions make one

both smile and wince. There is at least one of them, on average, every page. To read the book is to face epigrams and wisecracks and comic metaphors and satiric similes that constitute a verbal species of felonious assault. We laugh at them, and we also feel the pain, the morbidity, the essential unhappiness of those reformers. They are always ajar, nursing a pathological suspiciousness. They know the world is *bad*. For Olive Chancellor, "It was the usual things of life that filled her with silent rage; which was natural enough inasmuch as, to her visions, almost everything that was usual was iniquitous." But she is just as iniquitous as anybody else; she really does buy Verena from her father: "she expressed to herself the kind of man she believed him to be in reflecting that if she should offer him ten thousand dollars to renounce all claim to Verena, keeping—he and his wife—off her for the rest of time, he would probably say, with his fearful smile, 'Make it twenty, money down, and I'll do it.'" Olive goes right ahead in her purchase, and we can't tell which is more odious, her doing it (Olive, whom we take seriously) or the girl's manager-father (Selah, whom we don't) accepting it. Olive reflects that Verena "made a great sacrifice of filial duty in coming to live with her (this, of course, should be permanent—she would buy off the Tarrants from year to year)." The matter-of-factness is chilling.

Irving Howe declares that "for a writer who is often said to shy away from physical experience," in this novel James "seems remarkably aware of the female body"; Tony Tanner echoes that by saying "in no other of his novels does James pay more attention to the physical appearance of his characters." Mrs. Burrage is "a stout, elderly, ugly lady, dressed in brilliant color, with a twinkle of jewels and a bosom much uncovered," and "there were more twinkling, smiling ladies, with uncovered bosoms." Mrs. Luna, that grasping horse, is exhaustively described from her head to her "small fat foot." And James does to things what he does to his characters—backs of houses, interiors, gas lamps, Victorian drapery, and furniture. Everybody and everything are brutish and sweaty, too heavy and too near. In this world there is more glare than light. Every step in the plot promises fatality.

Nobody has described that plot better than Darrel Abel: as Verena "advances in her career of heralding the emancipation of women from the conjugal yoke, she progresses toward yielding herself in marriage to Ransom." It's a joke, a fight to the death, a tragedy, and nobody gets out of it unmarked. As Tanner puts it, "The note of deviancy and perversion is pervasive and touches nearly all of the characters. No one is sure what constitutes his or her identity, what his or her place is in society, what exactly is each one's sexuality and what it entails." The sexuality of Olive Chancellor?—four times she and Verena are called "the Bostonians." *The* Bostonians. Are they in what was once called a "Boston marriage?" And why do the two sisters, Olive Chancellor and Adeline Luna, hate each other so much? Is it perhaps because each is a creature with ravenous sexual appetite, Olive for women and Adeline for men? "Mrs. Luna was drawing on her gloves; Ransom had never seen any that were so long; they reminded him of stockings, and he wondered how she managed without garters at the elbows." What of Doctor Prance, "Spare, dry, hard," whom Ransom sees "as a perfect example of the 'Yankee female'?" "It was true that if she had been a boy she would have borne some relation to a girl." James is on a search-and-destroy rampage in Beantown, and the arbiters of that city's culture were saying, There he goes again!

When Verena takes Basil to Memorial Hall at Harvard she says, "It's a real sin to put up such a building, just to glorify a lot of bloodshed." But Basil thinks it is "the finest piece of architecture" he has ever seen and it springs up "majestic into the winter air." It is "consecrated to the sons of the university who fell in the long Civil War." Ransom feels that "it stands there for duty and honor, it speaks of sacrifice and example, seems a kind of temple to youth, manhood, generosity," the "white, ranged tablets, each of which, in its proud, sad clearness, is inscribed with the name of a student soldier." It fills Ransom with "gentleness, with respect, with the sentiment of beauty." We read it so, along with Ransom. His is the profound feeling that eludes Verena; she "would have pulled it down."

What politics, what idea of public life, is to be inferred here? That question pervades the entire book. Whose "side" is James on? What, pardon my French, does James "privilege," "valorize," and "foreground"? To take another example of this problem, where do we think James stands when Basil Ransom delivers, again to Verena, in New York's Central Park, his indictment of the age of reform?

The whole generation is womanized; the masculine tone is passing out of the world; it's a feminine, a nervous, hysterical, chattering, canting age, an age of hollow phrases and false delicacy and exaggerated solicitudes and coddled sensibilities, which, if we don't soon look out, will usher in the reign of mediocrity, of the feeblest and flattest, and the most pretentious that has ever been. The masculine character, the ability to dare and endure, to know and yet not fear reality . . . that is what I want to preserve, or rather, as I may say, to recover; and I must tell you that I don't in the least care what becomes of you ladies while I make the attempt!

Is this romantic blather? Apparently so, because James adds, immediately, "the poor fellow delivered himself of these narrow notions (the rejection of which by leading periodicals was not a matter for surprise)." James knows there is a hint of "moral tinsel" in Ransom's sensibility.

But does the "rejection" of "leading periodicals" really count against him? James knew what the leading periodicals had said about *his* work. And does Ransom's "narrow" view of things bring him down to the level of the reformers he so obviously and overwhelmingly puts beneath him? Irving Howe assumes so: "Ransom is as naively and thoroughly, if not as unattractively, the victim of a fanatical obsession as Olive Chancellor. Ransom is deeply entangled with his ideology as Olive with hers."

No, as I understand it, not for a minute. In both Ransom's thoughts at Memorial Hall and his speech in Central Park, I think Henry James is solidly behind his "hero." Nothing in the substance or the diction of these passages indicates James as a satirist or Ransom as a conservative blowhard. If Ransom were the man Howe describes, why would James have modeled his "rather reckless attempt to represent a youthful Southern" on an actual Southern senator, the marvelously named Lucius Quintus Cincinnatus Lamar. Why would James write to a friend in Washington that he was "delighted that the benevolent Senator should have recognized some intelligence of intention, some happy divination." James expresses his "very great pleasure to know that in the figure of Basil Ransom he (Lamar) recognized something human and Mississippian. His word is a reward." Howe's idea that the scales are evenly balanced, that there are two equal fanaticisms, cannot be supported either in the text or in James's ancillary writings about it.

To be sure, in the end Ransom uses "muscular force" to drag Verena away from Olive, and we can again hear the growling bully in *Blithedale,*

Hollingsworth, who said that if women get out of line, "I would call upon my own sex to use its physical force." But Basil Ransom has a lively sense of humor; half the time he speaks "with a laugh." Hollingsworth has no sense of humor whatsoever, only his *idée fixe,* which is a great deal more *fixe* than *idée.* Ransom can think about things and turn them into coherent argument (if only for *The Rational Review*), and we can't help sharing at least to some degree his impressive insights into every character he meets.

Verena is not nearly so slight as critics have made her out to be. Early on, she sees the situation with epigrammatic good humor: she says to Basil, "Why, sir, you ought to take the platform too; we might go round together as poison and antidote!" She is quite aware that "Olive desires not only justice but vengeance," and she squirms under Olive's accusations: "I don't think I ought to be suspected so much. Why have you a manner as if I had to be watched, as if I wanted to run away with every man that speaks to me?" Verena is a remarkably gifted young woman. To Basil Ransom she is certainly clear: Verena is "a vocalist of exquisite faculty, condemned to sing bad music." Everything's wrong with her words, nothing is wrong with her voice. To seduce her, Ransom has to convert her—"she was to burn everything she had adored; she was to adore everything she had burned."

In *The Bostonians,* as in *The Blithedale Romance,* the ideological *is* the sexual. The most complicated and painful example of it is Olive Chancellor. In all her encounters with Ransom she seems unwarrantedly rude and dismissive. Early on, "Ransom offered his hand in farewell to his hostess; but Olive found it impossible to do anything but ignore the gesture. She could not have let him touch her." Surely this affable Southerner has given her no cause to be so ugly. Ransom thinks, "If he should not come she should be annoyed, and if he should come she would be furious." He concludes, as do we, that with Olive Chancellor you can't win. Her sister says that Olive is "a female Jacobin" and she "would reform the solar system if she could get hold of it." James portrays Olive as "a spinster as Shelley was a lyric poet, or as the month of August is sultry." And eventually we realize that she is not really rude; she is absolutely helpless. Olive can't win anything because she is determined to lose everything. "The most secret, the most sacred hope of her nature was that she might some day have such a chance that she might be a martyr and die for something." Ransom sees it with exemplary clarity: "no one could help her: that was what made her tragic."

Daniel Aaron asks (and does not answer), "Is her crusade to redress the wrongs of women or the sublimation of lesbian desire?" Professor Howe reports students asking him, "Did James *know* Olive was a lesbian?" It's a queer question. Olive is a lesbian, of course she is—what is this nonsense about James not *knowing*? When he was mapping out the plot, he said to himself, "The relation of those two girls should be a study of one of those friendships between women which are so common in New England." He had just seen one when he had spent the better part of a summer living with his sister Alice and her "friend," Katherine Loring. James viewed the relationship as "a devotion so perfect and so generous" as to constitute "a gift of providence."

For a century now critics have been ambitious to "prove" James's homosexuality. So what happens when, as one critic puts it, he portrays Olive as "the victim of her own sexual preference"? James is both homophobic and gay. Is that possible? Well, to be sure it is, and some would say that that is how "the closet" got itself built. Still, the question, is Olive unhappy *because* she's gay?

James says "there are women who are unmarried by accident, and others who are unmarried by option, but Olive Chancellor was unmarried by every implication of her being." She is "a woman without laughter," who has "absolutely no figure" and "colorless hair." Her smile "might have been likened to a thin ray of moonlight resting upon the wall of a prison." She is often "panting like a hunted creature." Ransom wonders about "the emancipation of Olive Chancellor's sex (what sex was it, great heaven?)" Early on, we hear the male voices call to Olive and Verena standing on the winter porch, "You ladies had better look out, or you'll freeze together." Olive is forever apologizing for who she is and what she does, "I see it was my jealousy that spoke—my restless, hungry jealousy." What is wrong with the masculine "race"?—"There are gentlemen in plenty who would be glad to stop your mouth by kissing you!" There is fury and desperation and foul play in her voice when she says of Basil Ransom, "Hasn't he the delicacy of one of his own slave-drivers?" And at times she goes completely berserk, flinging herself on the couch, and moaning "that he didn't love Verena, he never had loved her, it was only his hatred of their cause that had made him pretend it . . . he hated her, he only wanted to smother her, to crush her, to kill her . . . it was not tenderness that moved him—it was devilish malignity."

Such deeply painful tantrums are far worse than the opening rude gestures. But, oddly enough, our feelings toward Olive have undergone a change. In the closing scenes we feel, more than her perversity, her profound suffering. It is foremost when we follow her helpless waiting at the Cape, where she spends "the violence of her terror, the eagerness of her grief." She is driven "to pace the shore in frenzy." In this scene we see how wrong-headed was the judgment of André Gide, who complained that Jamesian characters were "only winged busts, all the weight of flesh is absent, all the shaggy, tangled undergrowth; all the wild darkness. His characters have no souls."

Early on, Olive "liked to think that Verena, in her childhood had known almost the extremity of poverty, and there was a kind of ferocity in the joy with which she reflected that there had been moments when this delicate creature came near (if only the pinch had lasted a little longer) to literally going without food." These curious phrases, "liked to think," "ferocity of joy," and "if the pinch had only lasted a little longer" mean what they say and also mean, much more darkly, "*liked* to think," and "if *only*." Now, on the beach,

> Her eyes rested on the boats she saw in the distance and she wondered if in one of them Verena were floating to her fate. Olive almost wished that she might glide away forever, the very thought made her feel faint and sick. Olive's imagination hurried, with a bound, to the worst. She saw the boat overturned and drifting out to sea, and (after a week of nameless horror) the body of an unknown young woman, defaced beyond recognition, but with long auburn hair and in a white dress washed up in some faraway cove.

To underline what is going on here, James resorts to a rhetorical device unique in his work: three times we are told, "it was a kind of shame." "Distinctly, it was a kind of shame." "She wished to keep the darkness. It was a kind of shame."

And the worst is still to come. In the Music Hall Ransom sees, "prostrate, fallen over, her head buried in the lap of Verena's mother, the tragic figure of Olive Chancellor." Olive is "literally praying to her kinsman not to ruin, not to shame!" "Quivering," she wonders "what humiliation, what degradation, what sacrifice" is demanded. When Ransom last sees her, "upright in her desolation," he recognizes "her pale, glittering eyes straining forward, as if looking for death." Ransom knows that "the expression of her face" will be "a thing to remain with him forever." He sees Olive "on a barricade" in the French revolution and even as "the sacrificial figure of Hypatia, whirled through the furious mob of Alexandria." With that, *The Bostonians,* a book so full of rich comedy and deadly satire, achieves truly tragic resonance.

James described *The Bostonians* as "an attempt to show that I *can* write an American story." He said that he had asked himself "what was the most salient and peculiar point in our social life. The answer was: the situation of women, the decline of the sentiment of sex, the agitation on their behalf." But as the predominantly negative reviews came in, he wrote his brother, "I had the sense of knowing terribly little about the kind of life I had attempted to describe," a failing he had already diagnosed in *The Blithedale Romance* ("we get too much out of reality, and cease to feel beneath our feet the firm ground of an appeal to our own vision of the world—our observation"). And, a century before the phrase was invented, both Hawthorne and James were "politically incorrect." Their whole notion of the convergence between the public and the private realms was decidedly skeptical and conservative. Richard Brodhead has written that "James's reversion to the sense that all political stories are really love stories in disguise is related to his return to Hawthorne as a literary model." Both men see "the struggle for public social change as growing out of private emotional distress and as disguising the pursuit of private emotional goals." Coverdale puts it perfectly: "Women, however intellectually superior, seldom disquiet themselves about the rights or wrongs of their sex, unless their own individual affections chance to lie in idleness, or to be ill at ease. They are not natural reformers, but become such by the pressure of exceptional misfortune." The reforming impulse itself is pathological; it is merely a disguise, a public cover. One benign and poignant example is Verena's hope "that something really bad happened to" Basil Ransom, for if it had then she could "help herself to forgive him for so much contempt." Visionary schemes and practical reforms are doomed because they arise from the thwarted love lives of the schemers and reformers themselves.

In *The Bostonians* this comes clear in the big final scene at the Music Hall. It is lengthy, twenty-five pages, full of "the sound of several thousand people stamping with their feet and rapping with their umbrellas and sticks." Ransom can't get through or around a sardonic cop. And what could be more crushing than for Olive to hear Mrs. Farrinder say, "Well, Miss Chancellor, if this is the way you're going to reinstate our sex!" It is "as if Mrs. Farrinder's words had been a lash." Under Ransom's protection Verena escapes, but "though she is glad," Ransom sees that "beneath her hood she was in tears." James's last sentence leaves her that way: "It is to be feared that with the union, so far from brilliant into which she was about to enter, these were not the last she was destined to shed." Irving Howe predicts that they are going to live unhappily ever after.

Did James have to bring such a gloomy close to this five hundred-page novel? By way of a postscript I should like to examine a little pamphlet which Susan Foster, one of our most accomplished new Cornell Ph.D.s, has generously shared with me. Dated 1887, it was written by Celia B. Whitehead and presented to Elizabeth Cady Stanton "with New Year's greetings." It is called

ANOTHER CHAPTER
OF
"THE BOSTONIANS"
BY
HENRIETTA JAMES

In it Basil Ransom is exposed as a fraud and a cad; Verena goes back to Olive. In an introductory note Whitehead says, "Inasmuch as Mr. James left the hero and heroines of his remarkable story at the most interesting period of their existence it seemed good to me to take them up and write 'Another Chapter.' " Many paragraphs and sentences are verbatim from James, and when Whitehead comes out with her own sentimental and dull prose there is a jarring effect (humor is not her strong suit). Ransom's "muscular force" is "a new proof of man's selfishness," but it does not do Olive Chancellor any lasting damage. She had "dreamed she couldn't stand there before that audience and deliver that address." And, dear reader, would you believe it?—"She could and she did." Oh, that's what we like to hear. Even if it is impossible. "The audience sat spellbound." When Olive gets home and falls into bed she realizes "that in trying to prepare Verena for this work she had been preparing herself."

Meanwhile, in New York, Basil and Verena find an "authorized clergyman," and they give him five dollars to marry them. But alas, as soon as Verena becomes Ransom's "legal possession," he loses interest in her. The war was more fun than the victory, and soon they fall into "a lull, a blank, a dreadful nothingness that was oppressive to both." Their shabby lodgings anticipate those of Carrie and Hurstwood. Poor Basil thinks "of the life of luxury and ease he might have lived with Mrs. Luna." He returns to her. He simply leaves a note for Verena (now a mother as well as a wife), "telling her that he had gone to Europe with Mrs. Luna and that she would now be free to exercise her 'gift for public speaking.' " He is a bounder; he gives up on his ideas, gives up on his family; he was a fake all along. Verena reads in the newspapers "of Olive's success in the work planned for *her.*" Well, "a proud woman would have died sooner than go back to one she had so hurt; but we know Verena was not proud." So, "she went back, and found Olive with a desire to take her friend in her arms again on any terms—and the baby too." Verena knows she has done the right thing, she knows it "with the first touch of Olive's hand, the first kiss of her lips." Verena names her infant daughter "Olive." As for Ransom, "what a barbarian he had shown himself at the last—carrying her off bodily and forcibly, as a member of one of the wild tribes carries off a woman he wants for his." Eventually Verena becomes "ready to take up her old work"; things "had all turned out right after all." An unexpected benefit is young Mr. Burrage, who in *The Bostonians* had been presented as a dilettante who "collected enamels and Cremona violins." Now "his fondness for music had grown into a passion, and he was devoting himself for the love of it; even to the drudgery of teaching it." We remember his mother's clever appeal to Olive that he would make for their purposes a perfect husband, too weak to prevent Verena from continuing her great

Chapter Seven

The Great Stories

"Hawthorne and His Mosses" records Melville's euphoria about Nathaniel Hawthorne's short stories, not his novels. *The Scarlet Letter* had already been published, but we find no mention of it in "Mosses" or anywhere else in Melville's writing. He did write a letter to Hawthorne in April 1851, a sentimental, oddly cute paragraph about *The House of the Seven Gables*. But it was the short stories that inspired him. Reading them requires a rather special skill, and I should like to look very briefly at two ways not to do it, one from the Left and one from the Right, in so far as our aesthetic ideas have a political dimension. Judith Fetterley asserts that Hawthorne's "The Birthmark" is testimony "to the pervasive sexism of our culture. Most readers would describe it as a story of failure rather than as the success story it really is—the demonstration of how to murder your wife and get away with it. The only good woman is a dead one and the motive underlying the desire to perfect is the need to eliminate."

Fetterley seems to be quite oblivious to the story's obvious predication of perverse sexuality. We know from page 1 that it is fatal. It's a Frankenstein story, an attack on experimental science; Aylmer is a "vile empiric" like Rappaccini (about whom Hawthorne would write the following year). We could almost call it "a genre story," so frequently did Hawthorne write a version of it, as did many other, lesser writers of his time.

On the Right, as I would define it, Allen Tate curiously misreads the last paragraph of "Young Goodman Brown." He combines clichés of "creative writing" and downright wrong-headedness:

> The dramatic impact would have been stronger if Hawthorne had let the incidents tell their own story: Goodman Brown's behavior to his neighbors and finally to his wife *show* us that he is a changed man. Since fiction is a kind of shorthand of human behavior and one moment may represent years in a man's life, we would have concluded that the change was to last his entire life. But Hawthorne's weakness for moralizing and his insufficient technical equipment betray him into the anticlimax of the last paragraph.

I think it is precisely the last paragraph that hits the reader like the crack of doom. Tate prefers to have the story end with its brief penultimate paragraph: "Had Goodman Brown fallen asleep in the forest and only dreamed a wild dream of a witch meeting?" Hawthorne says, "Be it so, if you will; but, alas! it was a dream of evil omen for young Goodman Brown." And then he writes one of his most majestic sentences: "A stern, a sad, a darkly meditative, a distrustful, if not a desperate man did he become from the night of that fearful dream." One should hear— stunned, enraptured—that somber music. It is a perfect verdict, a death sentence, terrifying in its brevity: the Fool of Virtue has become the Fool of Vice. Even the Puritans themselves would have recognized it; they warned of "Inordinate Gloom."

Two of Hawthorne's greatest stories, "The Minister's Black Veil" (my own favorite) and "My Kinsman Major Molineux" were written early— "Veil" in 1835, and "Kinsman" even earlier, in 1829 (when Hawthorne was only twenty-five). He did not include either one in the *Twice-Told Tales* of 1837. "The Minister's Black Veil" had to wait for *Mosses from an Old Manse,* nearly a decade later (1846) and "My Kinsman" finally made it into the last collection of stories, *The Snow Image* (1852). The reason for the long delay, especially for the latter, is a problem I shall return to later, but first I want to ask a question about Hawthorne's subtitle for "The

Minister's Black Veil." He called it "A Parable," and my question is, simply, a parable of what? Hawthorne appended a footnote about "another clergyman in New England," who put a veil over his face—indeed, he was known as "Handkerchief Moody"—"in early life he had accidentally killed a beloved friend; and from that day till the hour of his own death, he hid his face from men." Hawthorne says that Moody's veil "had a different import" from the one on Parson Hooper. Different? No, it has an import—perhaps grief or guilt—but we never know what Parson Hooper's veil signifies, or why he puts it on, or what the "Parable" means. J. Hillis Miller notes that the black veil "is an ordinarily feminine article of clothing worn by a man." In the story itself, a lady remarks, "How strange that a simple black veil, such as any woman might wear on her bonnet, should become such a terrible thing on Mr. Hooper's face!" Miller writes: "Hooper is a weird kind of transvestite, weird because wearing the veil by no means feminizes him nor even makes him sexually neutral. He remains aggressively masculine, patriarchal." So patriarchal, I might add, that as the years wore on he acquired throughout New England churches the name "Father Hooper." Patriarchal indeed (and dangerously close to Catholic). Miller notes that

> even for Hooper, who lives behind the veil and should therefore know what it typifies, the sight of his veiled face (in a mirror) is terrifying. This is the case not because the veil signifies a secret guilt of which he is aware, nor because he knows that he consorts with the devil behind it—no textual support is given to these hypotheses. To say of the veil it is a symbol of sin, it is sorrow, it is madness, it is New England Puritanism in a Franklinian culture, or it is the cover for sexual secrets is to receive no response from the text. It says neither yes nor no to whatever hypotheses about it the reader proposes.

The very core and ultimate significance of the story is enigmatic. It is like that terrible facial expression Hawthorne uses quite often in his work—the smile. We watch that "melancholy smile"; we see that "Mr. Hooper's smile glimmered faintly"; later, "he even smiled again—that same sad smile"; and when death finally overtakes him, "Father Hooper fell back upon his pillow, a veiled corpse, with a faint smile lingering on the lips." What, we ask, does that smile *mean*? But the smile, like the veil itself, has only the meaning we ourselves assign to it. The story keeps its secrets to itself.

Frederick Crews knows what this is all about (or at least he used to, before he changed his team uniform): Mister Hooper put on the veil to avoid marriage, to avoid adult genital sexuality. Another Freudian is sure that the spilled glass of wine is premature ejaculation. I don't see why we need to get so diagrammatic about it. The story is very much about its time and place; Hawthorne shows us all the reactions in that tight little town: incredulity, fear, anger, hysteria. Hooper is one of those preachers like Dimmesdale who "strove to win his people heavenward, by mild persuasive influences, rather than to drive them thither by the thunders of the Word." He is passive, one of Hawthorne's most striking nonparticipants in the game of life, a man with a "painful degree of self-distrust" (Hawthorne's good friend, Horatio Bridge, who subsidized the publication of *Twice-Told Tales,* wrote to him, " 'The bane of your life has been self-distrust"). And we should remember that Hawthorne, during the "Lonely Chamber" period, 1825-1837, had in a sense worn the black veil himself for twelve years, living with his mother and sisters, indulging his "cursed habits of solitude."

So far, so good. "The Minister's Black Veil" is a story about pathological withdrawal, about a "bugbear" who "could not walk the street with any peace of mind." And "still good Mr. Hooper sadly smiled." But then we come to this absolutely astonishing sentence: "Among all its bad influences, the black veil had the one desirable effect, of making its wearer a very efficient clergyman." We are suddenly reminded that what seems like evasion is actually Hooper's most powerful action of his most sacred calling. He "became a man of awful power, over souls that were in agony for sin. Its gloom, indeed, enabled him to sympathize with all dark affections. Dying sinners cried aloud for Mr. Hooper, and would not yield their breath till he appeared." "Strangers came long distances to attend service at his church," and he is appointed to preach the election sermon. Yes, the veil had "kept him in that saddest of all prisons, his own heart," but in what mattered most to him—and to his parishioners—and to us—is that he had "wrought so late into the evening, and done his work so well."

Having taught this story for over thirty years, I notice that it never becomes boring; it is always new, and I don't so much remember my initial his rival for the woman's love is carrying a .38, "Mine's bigger than yours.") We have in Robin's dream, quite literally, a "family tree." As with Julian Sorel or Pip or David Copperfield, there is a portrait of city sexuality (here it is the woman in the scarlet petticoat). Robin turns her down; he is "of the household of a New England clergyman, and a good youth, as well as a shrewd one, so he resisted temptation, and fled away." The story picks up speed; it goes from random walk to running nightmare. And "the moon, 'creating like the imaginative power, a beautiful strangeness in familiar objects,' gave something of romance to a scene that might not have possessed it in the light of day." I have not yet been able to discover what those quotation marks are doing in there, and I do not know to what work he is referring (unless to his own). But that familiar definition of "Romance," as we have seen it in his prefaces, is not adequate for the most important revelation in the story: when Robin sees his kinsman, and sees what the town has done to him, "there the torches blazed the brightest, there the moon shone out like day." All the cackles and giggles and horse laughs come to a concluding outburst in which "every man shook his sides, every man emptied his lungs, but Robin's shout was the loudest there . . . as the congregated mirth went roaring up the sky!" We should understand this as Freudian, too, though in a slightly different way. Freud asked in *Jokes and the Unconscious* when it was that the first laugh went forth on this planet. Only Sigmund Freud could have asked that question, and only he could give it such a sinister answer: "After the first murder." That is what is happening here, a symbolic murder. "On they went, in counterfeited pomp, in senseless uproar, in frenzied merriment, trampling all on an old man's heart." It is a sentence as shocking as that one in "The Minister's Black Veil" about Hooper becoming "a very efficient clergyman." We are reminded of revolution's cost more than its necessity. "Counterfeited," "senseless," and "frenzied" do not endorse revolution; "trampling on an old man's heart" does not constitute patriotism.

When Robert Lowell made "My Kinsman" into the curtain raiser for *The Old Glory,* he presented it as a classical tragedy, the actors complete with masks and high platform shoes. Clearly the "father" in this story, as in *Oedipus,* stands blocking the road to the son's own adulthood. At the end we can turn the story inside out—Robin doesn't really want to find his father, that feeling is completely repressed and expresses itself only in displacement. Robin wants to see his "father" vanquished, and the boy's great shout erupts only when all his encounters with male authority suddenly become clear to him. Now he is a man. Earlier he had called the figure blocking his path "some country representative," that is, what Robin himself is. Throughout, Robin's experience has been one of suspicion, fear, and confusion, but now he knows himself in a new light, the true one. The boy still lives in the man, though, and at the very end he wants to quit: "I begin to grow weary of a town life, Sir. Will you show me the way to the Ferry?" He still needs a paternal hand to help him up, and he gets it, from his kindly companion: "No, my good friend, Robin, not to-night, at least . . . you may rise in the world, without the help of your kinsman, Major Molineux."

Both these fine stories show Hawthorne going over American history, searching for material. He once said he couldn't understand a newspaper unless it was a hundred years old. He needed to see "The Age" in a telling detail. Then he could make his own sense out of a little tatter of black cloth or a rambunctious Boston Tea Party.

The narrator of *The Aspern Papers* is altogether reliable, at least in the sense that, as F. W. Dupee says, he implicates "the reader in his plot to violate the past" and "it is at us as well as at the collector that Miss Bordereau hisses her climactic reproach, 'Ah, you publishing scoundrel!' " By that point in the story "we" want those letters, too. Our narrator is a very smart man; we take such pleasure in watching him work that his quest becomes ours.

But I mean "reliable" in the usual sense, too. Trustworthy. Dependable. Someone you can count on. Millicent Bell is right: "the first-person narrative imprisons us in indeterminacy," and "we remain unsure whether he may or may not have some claim upon our better opinion." I think he may. When James revised the story for the New York edition he made some extremely interesting changes. For example, "I had never said it to Tina Bordereau" becomes "I had never said it to my victim." Or in the sentence "I hadn't come back before night to contradict, even as a simple form, even as an act of common humanity, such an idea," the phrase "even as an act of common humanity" is new in the New York edition.

One can read these things as James condemning the unconscious narrator; one can also read them as the extremely conscious narrator condemning himself.

Philip Horne, in his splendid study of James's revisions, concludes that in this story "they involve us as readers in a sympathetic and ironic relation to the center of consciousness rather than a hostile and rampantly distrustful work of detection." In 1888 the story concluded, "When I look at it (the portrait of Aspern) my chagrin at the loss of the letters becomes almost intolerable." In the New York edition: "When I look at it I can scarcely bear my loss—I mean of the precious papers." The "—" is a masterstroke: its message is, Say, don't get the wrong idea!

Horne notes "the authorial inscrutability of the story"; still, he says, "the remembering self passes the action through a process of distancing and irony; the process works by the substantial restriction of the narration to a dramatization of past consciousness, the present narrator being as excluded as if he were another person. The story demonstrates his punishment for extravagant curiosity; the mode of its telling is thematically continuous with the action." The narrator's story is somewhere between a deeply embarrassed confession and an anguished apology. The narrator finally realizes that he had "unwittingly but none the less deplorably trifled."

James jotted down the "germ" of the story in Florence, in January 1887. Captain Silsbee, "the Boston art-critic and Shelley-worshipper" had had a "curious adventure" with "the niece of Miss Claremont, Byron's *ci-devant* mistress." James adheres to the anecdote's main outlines in *The Aspern Papers*. He changes the setting from Florence to Venice: happily, for the tale is filled with a sense of decay and the oppressive splendor of centuries past (James wrote the story in Venice, one of his most deeply loved cities). Miss Bordereau herself, Dupee asserts, "is no wistful survivor of the past but a diabolical incarnation of it, greedy of its power to bargain with the present." The narrator tells us that in devoting his life to Aspern he still "had not been able to look into a single pair of eyes into which his had looked, or feel a transmitted contact in any aged hand that his had touched." Fittingly, Juliana wears a green visor to hide her eyes, and she refuses to shake hands. But by the end of the story the narrator will see her "single pair of eyes" in a way that he will never forget. Here again the revisions are extremely important: the original, "I beheld her extraordinary eyes. They glared at me," becomes "I beheld her extraordinary eyes. They glared at me; they were like the sudden drench, for a caught burglar, of a flood of gaslight." In both, "they made me horribly ashamed."

I wonder what Freud would have done with this one. Some sentences I would not dream of touching: for examply, "I hadn't meanwhile meant by my private ejaculation that I must myself cultivate the tangled enclosure." More interesting, I think, is the story's parody of grand passion ("Miss Tina was not a poet's mistress any more than I was a poet"). The game is everywhere up for grabs—in "I felt almost as base as the reporter of a newspaper who forces his way into a house of mourning," the magic word is "almost." The pathetic and the heroic keep changing places, and sometimes they are identical ("She had hid them in her bed . . . between the mattresses"). And in the last paragraph, Miss Tina, "a plain dingy elderly person" has her revenge:

> "I've destroyed the papers. I burnt them last night, one by one, in the kitchen."
> "One by one?" I coldly echoed it.
> "It took a long time—there were so many."

Oh, dear! The story ends in exquisite dismay.

In the penultimate chapter of *The Tragic Muse* a painter sees in his great unfinished portrait that "the hand of time was rubbing it away little by little (for all the world as in some delicate Hawthorne tale), making the surface indistinct and bare of all resemblance to the model. Of course the moral of the Hawthorne tale would be that this personage would come back on the day when the last adumbration should have vanished." James was probably thinking of the "Prophetic Pictures" in *Twice-Told Tales*. Philip Horne suggests that the portrait-painter is possessed of "quasi-supernatural penetration" which " 'insulated him from the mass of human kind,' leaving him 'no aim,—no pleasure,—no sympathies.' "

For Hawthorne the artist is usually "chilly," at best, and this one is able to "predict the dark future" of his sitters. The darkest future of all, perhaps, is the artist's own.

And when I think of Hawthorne in connection with James's extraordinary novella *The Beast in the Jungle,* several things come to mind, two

Hawthorne stories in particular. The first is "The Christmas Banquet" with its brief headnote, "From the unpublished 'Allegories of the Heart.'" The central figure in the tale suffers from a "deficiency in his spiritual organization," the result of "a sense of cold unreality." Twice he is described as "Cold! Cold! Cold!" "'Who is this impassive man?' has been asked a hundred times. 'Has he suffered? Has he sinned? There are no traces of either.'" Talk about cold!—"His wife went to her grave, and was doubtless warmer there."

"John Marcher's arid end" is prefigured by the chief figure among the guests at the dismal annual feast when he says, "It is a chillness—a want of earnestness—a feeling as if what should be my heart were a thing of vapor—a haunting perception of unreality! I have really possessed nothing, neither joys nor griefs. All things have been like shadows flickering on the wall. Neither have I myself any real existence, but am a shadow like the rest."

Hawthorne concludes, "Of such persons—and we do meet with these moral monsters now and then—it is difficult to conceive how they came to exist here, or what there is in them capable of existence hereafter. They seem to be on the *outside* of everything" (my italics). John Marcher, we are told, "had seen *outside* of his life" (James's italics) "not learned it within," and at the end he stands in the graveyard "gazing at the sounded void of his life."

The other story I think of, one of Hawthorne's greatest, was written within months of "The Minister's Black Veil" (1835 was a good year for Hawthorne), "Wakefield." Although "Wakefield" and *The Beast in the Jungle* don't look much alike, they are profoundly connected; in both a man turns away from the woman in his life, and lives many years without her but very close to her. Jorge Luis Borges is especially insightful here:

> In general, situations were Hawthorne's stimulus, his point of departure—situations, not characters. Hawthorne first imagined, perhaps unwittingly, a situation and then sought the characters to embody it. I am not a novelist, but I suspect that few novelists have proceeded in that fashion. Hawthorne's stories are better than Hawthorne's novels, I believe that is true. The twenty-four chapters of *The Scarlet Letter* abound in memorable passages, written in good and sensitive prose, but none of

them has moved me like the singular story of "Wakefield" in *The Twice-Told Tales.*

Borges adds, "In that brief and ominous parable, which dates from 1835, we have already entered the world of Herman Melville." That is true; just before he composed "Bartleby" Melville wrote to Hawthorne about "your London husband." Oddly enough, what moves Borges the most is "the protagonist's profound *triviality,* which contrasts with the magnitude of his perdition," a phrase that applies equally well to both Wakefield and John Marcher.

Hawthorne begins by telling us he recollects a story "in some old magazine or newspaper"—there again is that hundred-year-old newspaper—"perhaps the strangest instance on record of marital delinquency." There is a puzzling problem in these stories about absentee husbands: what are their motives? Wakefield withdraws "without the shadow of a reason for such self-banishment." Hawthorne speaks of "the vagueness of the project," and says, "he had contrived or rather he had happened, to dissever himself from the world." He bears a family resemblance to Father Hooper, Coverdale, and Dimmesdale, as if he were their elder brother or uncle. "He was intellectual, but not actively so," possessed of "a mind never perplexed with originality," and "a quiet selfishness that had rusted into it." His "triviality" is apparent in his "long and lazy musings that ended to no purpose, or had not vigor to attain it. Imagination, in the proper meaning of the term, made no part of Wakefield's gifts." We first meet him as he prepares to take off for twenty years: it is in "the dusk of an October evening. He has an umbrella in one hand." In the fourth paragraph we encounter that Hawthorne trademark smile; four times in ten lines: Wakefield bids his wife goodbye, but "after the door has closed behind him, she perceives it thrust partly open, and a vision of her husband's face, smiling through the aperture." She dismisses this incident without a thought, "but long afterwards, when she has been more years a widow than a wife, that smile recurs." It is "the original smile." As with Father Hooper, "if she imagines him in a coffin, that parting look is frozen on his pale features"; and "if she dreams of him in heaven, still his blessed spirit wears a quiet and crafty smile."

On the day after he makes his getaway, when Wakefield prowls the street in his "morbid vanity," he is not found out; he is almost delirious in his happiness: "wonderful escape!" In *The Scarlet Letter,* when Hester in the forest takes off her badge, it, too, is a wonderful escape—"Oh, exquisite relief!" (Years later, still unrecognized, Wakefield "hurries to his lodgings, bolts the door, and throws himself upon the bed. The latent feelings of years break out." Again, as in *The Scarlet Letter's* forest scene, Hawthorne's characteristic habit of mind is to balance stiff public rigidity with languid private luxuriance.) Wakefield hovers for years, watching, watching. Wakefield can always go back. " 'It is but in the next street!' he sometimes says," but Hawthorne growls at him, "'Fool! it is in another world.'" Hawthorne asserts that "an influence beyond our control lays his strong hand on every deed which we do, and weaves its consequences into an iron tissue of necessity." This is original sin in classic Christianity (and, we might add, in classic Freud). The terror of the situation is that Wakefield "was, we may figuratively say, always beside his wife and at his hearth" and "still involved in human interests, while he had lost his reciprocal influence on them." It is a nightmare of impotence, a deep circle in Dante's hell, "proximity without intimacy."

One can also read it, I think, as twenty years in a snap of the fingers, the anatomy of a moment; at the very end of the story we see Wakefield just as he was at the very beginning: it is still "a gusty night of autumn" and he is carrying his umbrella. It could be called a "what if?" story. And we see the same "crafty smile." It takes a split second. A trivial man becomes "the Outcast of the Universe."

Before looking closely at *The Beast in the Jungle* I should clarify my rather loosely defined use of "Freudian." What I mean, of course, is neo-Freudian, the flag under which some modern critical ships sail. Sigmund Freud is one of the most challenging and powerful art critics I have ever read, and his essays on Leonardo, Michelangelo, Sophocles, Shakespeare, and Dostoevsky, among others, are works of genius. Anticipating the abuses of his ideas, Freud himself eloquently insisted that "the author cannot yield to the psychiatrist." Freud urged the psychoanalytical critic not to "coarsen everything" with the "substantially useless and awkward terms" of clinical analysis. "The layman," Freud said, "may expect perhaps too much from analysis, for it must be admitted that it throws no light upon the two problems which probably interest him the most. It can do nothing toward elucidating the nature of the artistic gift, nor can it explain the means by which the artist works—artistic technique." The approach can be dangerously reductive; it leads us away from the actual terms of a work of art to its latent terms, where the question is no longer "what does it mean?" but rather "what does it *really* mean?" Freud asserts the need for a most careful definition and investigation of how a culture relates to individual fantasies and how our private nightmares are expressive of the culture in which we live. There is a severe moral and intellectual danger in the insistence that all life or artistic work must be carted back to some primal bed where all our "real" encounters take place. Most neo-Freudians, it seems to me, do not provide an adequate sense of the complexity or the moral urgency a great work can give us.

The worst psychoanalytical piece of work on James that I have encountered is Maxwell Geismar's *Henry James and the Jacobites*. The book is one long, sustained exercise in name-calling; James was "ignorant, improvised, unjust, patronizing above all to the American scene and deliberately ingratiating, at once fawning and snobbish." Geismar says "Mme. Merle is the old-world magician, as her name indicates"—but clearly Merle isn't shorthand for Merlin; no, a "merle" is a European blackbird (and migratory, too). Howells once said that some readers simply couldn't respond to the work of Henry James, and they seemed to "want to have it out with him personally, even pugilistically." That is what Geismar does: "Henry James would have found in Hitler a St. George." Geismar says of *The Beast in the Jungle* that "the central concept of love here was that of devouring or being devoured—this infantile-oral, pre-oedipal or pre-sexual fantasy of love and sex in terms of food and cannibalism." When I quoted this verdict to my mentor, Fred Dupee, he said with that wonderful grin of his, "Oh, that makes it sound much more interesting than it really is."

Far more "interesting" than Geismar is the brilliant work of Eve Kosofsky Sedgwick, a Cornellian and a prominent figure in the "Queer Theory" movement; she is not so much a psychoanalytic critic as she is a specialist in gay and gender criticism. In her famous essay, "The Beast in the Closet," she proposes that James is an example of "The Writing of Homosexual Panic." John Marcher "lives as one who is *in the closet*. His angle on daily existence and intercourse is that of the closeted person."

Sedgwick takes special note of James's phrase "a long act of dissimulation," and cites "lexical pointers to a homosexual meaning":

> The rest of the world of course thought him *queer,* but she (May Bartram), she only, knew how, and above all why, queer; which was precisely what enabled her to dispose the concealing veil in the right folds. She took his *gaiety* from him—since it had to pass with them for *gaiety*—as she took everything else. . . . She traced his unhappy *perversion* through reaches of its course into which he could scarce follow it.

Sedgwick says, "emphasis added." But it is not "emphasis added"; it is emphasis invented. "Queer" and "gaiety" did not mean in 1903 what they mean today. Sedgwick does not so much interpret a text as she wishes "to crack a code and enjoy the reassuring exhilarations of knowingness, to buy into the specific formula, 'We Know What That Means.' " She complains that critics who do not endorse her view "know about the male-erotic pathways of James's personal desires," but "appear to be untroubled about leaving them out of accounts of his writing."

At least a couple of these objections seem to me badly out of line. I don't claim to know very much about the specifics of James's sex life; I agree with Millicent Bell's conclusion that it was a sex life of "zero manifestation." Critics who read James's letters and base their argument on them usually do not take into account the late Victorian tradition of formulary sentimentalism. James loved to write in that style. It's gush. A few readers of my novel *Beecher* have asked me if the character Theodore Tilton was homosexual, because he wrote such rhapsodic, flowery letters to Henry Ward Beecher (in fact, Tilton seems to have suffered from a thoroughly heterosexual case of satyriasis). The patches of purple prose are examples, to my mind, of a conscious extravagant convention in which strong friendship sounds like romantic love.

And I wonder—granting that to speak plainly in print was impossible—why in both notebook entries about *The Beast in the Jungle,* February 1895 and August 1901, the story presented itself to James, in his most private ruminations, as resolutely heterosexual, predicated on the two characters being a man and a woman. And why would Henry James, "the historian of fine consciousness," compose such a long story about a gay man hiding in the closet, too repressed even to guess at his own sexual preference? That rather dim and obvious *donnée* doesn't promise much imaginative reward.

Second, Sedgwick charges that critics who don't see the story her way are homophobic, willfully misreading and consciously suppressing something they know to be true. On the contrary, I do not *know* what she says not to be true, I just cannot find it in the story. When we study Walt Whitman, especially poems such as "I Sing the Body Electric" or "I Saw in Louisiana a Live Oak Growing," failure to recognize the speaker's homosexuality results in an impoverished misreading of his poetry. But I don't think Sedgwick tells me what I can't or don't want to hear; I think she tells me something false. For example, she writes that at the great culminating scene in the London cemetery, where Marcher sees genuine grief in another mourner's face, "Whitmanian cruisiness seems at first to tinge the air." Oh, surely that is not so. "Whitmanian cruisiness?" This grief-stricken man? Sedgwick says, "What is strikingly open in 'The Beast in the Jungle' is a man's desire for a man—and the denial of that desire." Sedgwick says that May Bartram sees Marcher's problem and attempts to assist him in bringing his homosexuality to full consciousness. But if that is true, Miss Bartram certainly has a very weird way of doing so. To the end she constantly offers herself sexually to him. Sedgwick's argument is self-contradictory: "I know you're gay, so sleep with me." April is the cruelest month; on that April day what May Bartram actually said to Marcher was, "The door's open!" as she "showed herself, all draped and all soft, in her fairness and slimness." She said to him, "It's never too late." Marcher couldn't hear her not because he's gay but because he's emotionally deaf.

Little Bilham in *The Ambassadors* is surely homosexual. James knows it; Strether seems to miss it completely. When he bursts out, "Live all you can; it's a mistake not to. It doesn't so much matter what you do in particular, so long as you have your life. Live!" and strives to set up Bilham with the Pocock girl, poor Bilham can only say, archly, "Oh, my dear man!" The fundamental sexual ignorance of Strether leads to a comic result; in the case of John Marcher it leads to a tragic one. *The Beast in the Jungle* is a terribly, utterly painful story, a truly great story. It is also one of the most ridiculous stories ever written, its style vague (no "solidity of specification" here) and its "hero" completely inadequate, oblivious, unresponsive to any real demand. Max Beerbohm's wonderful parody is "The Mote in the Middle Distance": the beast in this jungle is Santa Claus and the two watchers are a little boy and a little girl whispering to each other in bed on Christmas morning, wondering whether the Santa Beast has, as it were, come. Beerbohm has James's style, especially his dialogue, precisely. The parody shows us that the original teeters on the edge of the absolutely absurd.

I often ask my students, "Why can't you simply say that John Marcher is repressed; he can't love because he's too timid to do so; he's afraid of S-E-X. What is inaccurate about that?" We note the deeply sexual imagery everywhere in the story, all the puns on "coming violence," "intercourse," "penetrating," "climax," "exposed," "conceive." "He rose" to "the long avenue," this "powerless" man "spending himself" "so deep down that he winced at the steady thrust" "to drive the truth home." When Marcher thinks of the spring of the beast as "possibly destroying, possibly annihilating me," "altering everything, striking at the root of all my world," James uses the language of sex traditionally, as our culture talks about it; May Bartram sees it as "the sense of danger, familiar to so many people— of falling in love." Of course! The entire story centers on images of orgasm (or just the moment before, when you are in control and completely out of control at the same time), "like a crouching beast in the jungle it signified little whether the crouching beast were destined to slay him or to be slain, the definite point was the inevitable spring of the creature." The Beast *is* Sexual Responsiveness—we are true to the literal terms of the story to say that. It is a nightmare of hideous incapacity.

At this point I could hardly blame my reader for saying, "How can you begrudge Sedgwick her puns? You are doing the same thing—it's just that she does it homosexually and you do it heterosexually." To which I might reply with my fear that "cracking a code" turns the story into the question is he or isn't he? The answer doesn't much matter; it's the question that's wrong. Not as trivial as a parlor game, it is a game nonetheless: we "solve" the story instead of reading it. In both Freudian, psychoanalytic criticism and in typical gay/gender analysis the motivating idea and the rhetorical vocabulary cannot convey the intensity and imaginative power; the aim is emotionally narrow and falsely conclusive. I remember with pleasure a young man in my Melville seminar one year who came up with a triple-threat definition: "There is heterosexual sex, homosexual sex, and genius sex—great writers eroticize everything."

John Marcher's beast in the jungle is not a "Tyger, tyger burning bright in the forests of the night"; he is wondering, "Do I dare to eat a peach?" The beast is the fear of sex itself, fear of life, fear of the darkly lush, fear of being helplessly involved in that which may claim you. John Marcher realizes it at the end. Now he knows, and "everything fell together, confessed, explained, overwhelmed; leaving him most of all stupefied."

> The Beast, at its hour, had sprung; it had sprung in that twilight of the cold April when ashen, pale, ill, wasted, but all beautiful, and perhaps then recoverable, she had risen from her chair to stand before him . . . it had sprung as he didn't guess; it had sprung as she hopelessly turned from him.

The great event had happened, and Marcher was so self-involved he couldn't see it. Now he does—"*Too late!*" Sedgwick seems to me "wrong" in her specifics but surely right in reminding us to read the tale as one of James's greatest ghost stories, about the sex not had, about the feeling not ventured. The emotion is not regret but terror—the title says it all. And finally Marcher goes down, goes all the way with May Bartram: their bridal chamber is a tomb. Kierkegaard wrote, "Once there was a man so abstracted from his own existence that he awoke one morning to find himself dead."

Borges's remark quoted earlier, on the "triviality" of Wakefield applies grimly and perfectly to John Marcher as well. James shows us Marcher's crushing final realization, that he is "to have been the one man in the world to whom nothing whatever was to happen." Matthiessen comments, "That statement could very well have come from Hawthorne's notebooks." *The Beast in the Jungle* is "again a token of James's enduring kinship with Hawthorne." John Marcher illustrates Hawthorne's bewildered cry, "I have not lived but only dreamed of living!" Stephen Donadio argues that in

> both Hawthorne and James, there is a persistent fear that the tendency
> to read experience (individual or collective) like a text in order to ex-

tract symbolic meanings from it—a habit of mind ultimately associated with Puritanism—will become so all-consuming that the most pressing realities of one's existence, the nearest possibilities, will be rendered insubstantial and ungraspable. John Marcher spends most of his time staring his fate (in the person of May Bartram) in the face and failing to get the point precisely because it is so apparent.

F. W. Dupee makes an epigram out of it: "Marcher is an Ethan Brand who has read Walter Pater."

The Beast in the Jungle is a genre tale that belongs securely in the tradition of Hawthorne and is at the same time a striking instance of James's modernity. James says of John Marcher, after May Bertram dies, "The lost stuff of consciousness became thus for him as a strayed or stolen child to an unappeasable father; he hunted it up and down very much as if he were knocking at doors or enquiring of the police." Dupee is entirely persuasive here: "Among the writers of Joyce's and Kafka's generation the 'as if' becomes 'is.' " James's elaborate metaphors and similes become the narrative itself: figures of speech become plot.

Max Beerbohm, "Mr. Henry James." Photo Ashmolean Museum, Oxford.
Reproduced by permission of Sir Rupert Hart-Davis.

Chapter Eight

Ghosts

Millicent Bell says, "Contemporary records indicate that in the 1840s—the period in which 'The Turn of the Screw' seems to be set—governesses accounted for the single largest category of female patients in English asylums for the insane." That is, whatever is troubling the young lady who tells us the story appears to be an occupational hazard. She has a lot of company.

We should look at the emotional state the governess is in just before the ghosts appear to her. Prior to seeing Peter Quint, she finds herself "under a charm," "lifted aloft on a great wave of infatuation and pity." She says her feeling is "actually like the spring of a beast" (!). She saunters along in the garden of Bly, and she loves it because "it was a pleasure at these moments to feel myself tranquil and justified; doubtless perhaps also to reflect that by my discretion, my quiet good sense and general high propriety, I was giving pleasure—if he ever thought of it!—to the person to whose pressure I had yielded." That "he," that "person," is, of course, her employer. She says, "Well, I needed to be remarkable." She wishes that "some one would appear there at the turn of a path and would stand before me and smile and approve. I didn't ask more than that—I only asked that he should *know*." And suddenly her "imagination had, in a flash, turned real. He did stand there!" But she fears what she wants; she instinctively knows that it is not right for her to engineer "the fine machinery I had set in motion to attract his attention to my slighted charms." So in her fantasy she projects a "bad" master. She hates and fears what she desires, and the figure embodies her double feeling. Quint is sexually powerful, murderously so; she must be drawn to him and repudiate him at the same time. Quint does double duty: his appearance tells her that her urgency is justified—as one reader puts it, "the supreme heroism she wants to demonstrate in behalf of the children demands a supreme danger to them."

Quint is the Devil. The governess is a parson's daughter, well-acquainted with this man and his curly red hair, "it was just as if I had been looking at him for years and had known him always." "He's tall, active, erect—but never—no, never a gentleman." Anthony Curtis claims that "Quint may owe much to the figure of George Bernard Shaw, a professed non-gentleman, sporter of a red beard, and a rival of James in the theatre. Shaw was a campaigner for the work of Ibsen, whose *Peer Gynt* sounds suspiciously like 'Peter Quint.'" To my ear, though, the stronger echo is Shakespearean—a much likelier allusion for James to make, "Peter Quince" in *A Midsummer's Night Dream*. (But why either one?) The hatless ghost, at any rate, had died of a blow to the head when he was drunk; and sex in this story is drunk, sex is intoxicating—but inebriation is also brutal, it is deadly—no wonder the governess never sees Quint below the waist. James, of course, could not explicitly say any of this; as William Lyon Phelps asserted, "had he spoken plainly the book might have been barred from the mails." Perverse sexuality was certainly on James's mind—just before writing the tale he had been immersed in the Byron papers, "masses of ancient indecency" about incest, severe sexual disorder in the family. This could be Exhibit A in creating a case arguing the governess's delinquency and shaky sanity.

Second, you could indict her because she does not fight for Miles at school; she simply accepts his expulsion, and doesn't ask the headmaster for explanations; his letter "can have but one meaning." Only one? And what is that? She blackmails poor Miles; the more she comes to know him he is for her "a revelation of the possibilities of beautiful intercourse." In the quasi "Custom-House" introductory (authenticating the story, bound in red and gilt-edged), we find that Douglas was in love with her when he was ten years her junior, and in the narrative itself

Miles is ten and the governess twenty. Consider the way the governess makes love to Miles—no wonder the little fellow blows out the candle. We sympathize with his desire to get away from this lady—who thinks, before she scares him to death, that they're a couple on the verge of consummating their marriage: "we continued silent while the maid was with us—as silent, it whimsically occurred to me, as some young couple, who, on their wedding-journey, at the inn, feel shy in the presence of the waiter." The governess doesn't try to get a new school for Miles; he wants one desperately, he wants to know more about life, especially guys, but that is just what she does not want him to know, she wants to hold on to him and keep him hers.

She is really pathetic. And dangerous. When she sees Flora and Mrs. Grose "united, as it were, in shocked opposition to me," Flora says, "I see nobody. I see nothing. I never have." Note those last three words—they prove the governess has been harassing her charges with her visions. Miles later speaks of "this queer business of ours" and "all the rest!" If the governess calls the children's uncle, Miles says, "You'll have to tell him— you'll have to tell him a tremendous lot!"

The "thread" of this screw is mental disorder. Edmund Wilson put it all together in 1934, in his famous essay "The Ambiguity of Henry James." Following a lead by Edna Kenton, he concluded that "the young governess who tells the story is a neurotic case of sex repression, and the ghosts are not real ghosts at all but merely the hallucinations of the governess." When I read *The Turn of the Screw,* I find it difficult to ignore that thesis; Wilson says, "there is never any real reason for supposing that anybody but the governess sees the ghosts." The children deny seeing them, and Mrs. Grose denies it, too. Wilson adds, "Observe also from the Freudian point of view, the significance of the governess's interest in the little girl's pieces of wood": the governess says that Flora "had picked up one which happened to have in it a little hole that had evidently suggested to her the idea of sticking in another fragment that might figure as a mast." Wilson notes, "the male apparition first appears on a tower and the female apparition on a lake."

Of great significance, surely, is that James did not include *The Turn of the Screw* with his other ghost stories in the New York edition; rather, he included it in volume 12, with stories of quite another kind, *The Aspern*

Papers, "The Liar," and another one called "The Two Faces." James couldn't be more clear about his governess's unreliability.

To interrupt for a moment, I would respond that to name something is not to understand it. "Sex repression"—what does that really tell us? I find the tower and the lake and the pieces of wood rather too obviously formulary and tiresome; far more interesting to me is that the second time the governess sees each ghost she puts herself where the ghost had been the first time, and puts the ghost where she had been. Too, that nobody else sees the ghosts does not prove that the ghosts are unreal; ghosts can make themselves visible only to those people they want to be seen by. In *Hamlet* Gertrude cannot see the ghost.

These questions would be easy to answer by those who accept Wilson's ideas. First, William James was president for two years of the Society for Psychical Research, and among its publications was the story of a spectral woman corrupting the mind of a child. On one occasion, a paper by Willy on "Observations of Certain Phenomena of Trance" was read aloud to the society by Harry. Francis S. Roellinger argues that "if James did not 'base' his story on the published reports of the Society, they might nevertheless have been a logical source of suggestions."

I have saved the biggest gun for last. Most compelling is Oscar Cargill's "Henry James as Freudian Pioneer," an astonishing paper on Breuer and Freud's *Studies in Hysteria,* in particular "The Case of Miss Lucy R.," which is clearly a source for *The Turn of the Screw.* Some people say there is no evidence that James read *Studies in Hysteria,* and they're right, but only if they ignore many clear signals, both internal and external, that he did.

Lucy R. came to Freud for treatment in 1891. She was a governess in Vienna, in charge of two children, "an English lady of rather delicate constitution" who was severely depressed and "tormented by subjective sensations of smell," especially burnt pastry. She said there had been a disaster in the kitchen when she was trying to teach the children a little about cooking. A letter had come from her mother in Glasgow, and the children took her answering letter; they scuffled, and she forgot about the bread. Freud wondered aloud that such a small event could disturb her so greatly. When he pressed Lucy R. on it she volunteered that her mother's letter said there was trouble at home; her mother needed her and wanted her back. Second, the governess said the other servants thought her "too proud for my position, and they united in intriguing against me and told the guardian of the children all sorts of things about me."

Freud reports:

> I told her I did not believe all these things (exceptional attachment for the children and sensitiveness toward other persons of the household) were simply due to her affection for the children. I thought she was rather in love with the master, perhaps unwittingly; she nurtured the hope of taking the place of the dead mother, and it was for that reason that she became so sensitive towards the servants. She feared lest they would notice something of her hope and scoff at her. She answered in her laconic manner: "Yes, I believe it is so."—"But if you knew you were in love with the master, why did you not tell me so?"—"But I did not know it, or rather I did not wish to know it. I wished to crowd it out of my mind, never to think of it."

She went on to say it wasn't her love she was ashamed of, but she was upset because she feared ridicule for falling in love with a man who was her employer, so rich, and so socially prominent. And she had fallen for him after a single job interview. After that she received only distant scoldings.

The smells that bothered her maybe weren't just burned pastry; or, rather, she thought that was the smell, but after several sessions Freud concluded that she had made a symbolic substitution. It was really cigar smoke. After dinner one evening a visitor who had been puffing on a cigar kissed the children, and their father became enraged. Also, earlier, a lady had kissed both children on the lips, which likewise made the father extremely angry. Freud reports that the governess said the father threatened to fire her, and both incidents occurred while she believed herself loved and was waiting for a repetition of their earlier serious and friendly talk. Freud was able to bring Lucy R. around; her neurosis was cured, and she lost this distressing obsession with smells of burnt pastry (and, I guess, went around for the rest of her life smelling cigar smoke).

I have reproduced Professor Cargill's study at some length here because thirty-five years after it first appeared in print, critics still dismiss it or otherwise denigrate it because there is no solid proof that James read it. No solid proof? On internal evidence alone:

1. Both Lucy R. and the governess at Bly become infatuated with their employers based on a single interview (well, all right, in James, two interviews).
2. There are two children to be cared for, a boy and a girl.
3. Peter Quint and Miss Jessel are the cigar smoker and the lady who kisses the children on the lips. Both Lucy R. and the governess are berated for letting a man and a woman get too close to their charges, that is, letting a suspicious man and a suspicious woman contaminate a little boy and a little girl.
4. All those letters—in both stories a governess is asked by her mother to return to help with trouble at home, and in both stories the children steal one of the letters.
5. James's governess has a keen sense of smell; she detects *baked bread* (!) in the housekeeper's room, and is forever going on about "the fragrance of purity" in the children.

External evidence is abundant, too. James's sister, Alice, went to England with him and was treated there by several English alienists. Some used hypnotism to rid her of "all hideous nervous distress" (she seems to have been obsessed with reports about the sexual habits of Eton schoolboys). Alice was treated by the French doctor J. J. Charcot, with whom William James and Freud himself had studied. Alphonse Daudet, Henry's friend, dedicated *L'Evangeliste* to Charcot, and Henry used that novel for *The Bostonians* (Olive Chancellor was derived from Madame Autheman in *L'Evangeliste*). The first notice in English of *Studies in Hysteria* was by F. W. H. Meyers, a good friend of both Henry and William.

My only objection to Professor Cargill's fine research is to his conclusion. He says that "Miss Kenton and Edmund Wilson were profoundly right in their characterization of the governess: there are no 'ghosts' in the story—the phantoms are creations of an hysterical mind, they are hallucinations." To think that way is, to my mind, to miss completely the power of the story. A dull student once complained that "nobody believes in ghosts anymore," and I asked "If you don't believe in ghosts, how can you read the story at all?" Is the governess "reliable"? Of course she is. If you don't believe in ghosts anymore how do you read that talkative apparition in *Hamlet,* if he isn't the "ghost" of Hamlet's father? In *The Turn of the Screw* those are *real ghosts.* Quint and Miss Jessel actually lived there, on that estate, and they really damaged real children, and the damage of their presence lingers. The governess didn't *make that up*—unless she made everything up—in which case she is Henry James. And he certainly had no enthusiasm for "the mere modern 'psychical' case—"washed clean of all queerness as by exposure to a flowing laboratory tap, and equipped with credentials vouching for this—the new type clearly promised little, for the more it was respectably certified the less it seemed of a nature to rouse the dear old sacred horror."

Let us look at passages by two fine critics who are not talking about *The Turn of the Screw* but whose arguments apply perfectly to it (both men are talking about *The Portrait of a Lady*). Please keep the governess in mind when we look at the following quotations from Philip Rahv and Yvor Winters. In "The Heiress of All the Ages," Rahv asserts that a young American woman is James's favorite heroine, a " 'passionate pilgrim' whose ordinary features are those of a good American bewildered in the presence of the European order." She succeeds in life by adjusting Europe to herself and herself to Europe. Failure is "either the loss of one's moral balance or the recoil into a state of aggrieved innocence." In Jamesian comedy the young woman

> responds "magnificently" to the beauty of the old-world scene even while keeping a tight hold on her native virtue: the ethical stamina, good will, and inwardness of her own provincial background. And thus living up to her author's idea both of Europe and America, she is able to mediate, if not wholly resolve, the conflict between the two cultures, between innocence and experience, between the sectarian code of the fathers and the more 'civilized' though also more devious and dangerous code of the lovers.

In *The Turn of the Screw* all this is turned again. Triumph is turned into defeat, failing the specific terms of what the triumph's achievement would require. The governess cannot reconcile the conflict between the father's code and the lover's code because she has them all mixed up, and in doing so she creates the ultimate harm. A little Puritan herself, she takes the father's code to a berserk extreme while operating under the spell of the lover's code.

Yvor Winters in "Maule's Well, or Henry James and the Relation of Morals to Manners," begins by summarizing James's leading idea, his master plan:

> there is a moral sense, a sense of decency, inherent in human character at its best; that this sense of decency, being only a sense, exists precariously, and may become confused and even hysterical in a crisis; that it may be enriched and cultivated through association with certain environments; that such association may, also, be carried so far as to extinguish the moral sense. This last relationship is that of the moral sense to an environment which may up to a certain point enrich it and beyond that point dissolve it.
>
> If we carry these generalizations a little farther into the special terms of his novels, we find that the moral sense as James conceives it is essentially American or at least appears to James most clearly in American character; that it can be cultivated by association with European civilization and manners; that it may be weakened or in some other manner betrayed by an excess of such association.

Again, this general idea applies perfectly to *The Turn of the Screw*. The governess comes from a rural parson's house (America) to Bly (stately Europe), where her repressive background and choked emotion force her to be decisive in a social arena she does not understand and is singularly ill-equipped to deal with. She becomes "hysterical in a crisis" through contact with the manners of a decadent system.

The image of a young heroine encountering what James calls her "predecessor, a woman seated with her back presented to" us could apply equally well both to Miss Jessel and to Mme. Merle—and she who sees her could be the governess or Isabel Archer. A naive "American" virgin encounters an elegant "European" sexual adventuress. It is one of James's most exciting encounters, one he turns to repeatedly, a central Jamesian moment.

Just above I called the governess a "little Puritan," and I see her as an extreme type of that breed, a pathological and authoritarian version; she is sure that *others* are sick and evil; she sees herself as one of God's elect, intended to fight and run the world on Christian principles. She is a Calvinist: people are saved or damned, innocent or deeply deceptive. No two ways about it, or should I say, *only* two ways about it; the governess feels, with every ounce of her being "the duty of resistance to extravagant fancies" and it must therefore follow that Miles and Flora are the opposite of what they seem: "their absolutely unnatural goodness is a policy and a fraud!" And why? The governess says to Mrs. Grose, "They're not mine—they're not ours. They're his and they're hers!"

When *The Turn of the Screw* was published, an enthusiastic reviewer for the *Athenaeum* said it "would have made even Hawthorne envious on his own ground." In "Young Goodman Brown," at the beginning of the story everyone is saved, and at the end everyone is damned. Hawthorne wrote to Sophia Peabody, "I have really thought sometimes that God gave you to me to be the salvation of my soul." That is what Young Goodman Brown thinks of his wife, his "Poor little Faith." The governess dreams about the master and then suddenly sees him; Young Goodman Brown wonders, "What if the devil himself should be at my very elbow," and immediately beholds "the figure of a man" who is clearly Satanic. Brown says, "My father never went into the woods on such an errand," and the Devil quickly disabuses him of that idea by reciting highly sexual and brutal examples of both his father and grandfather doing the Devil's work (both figures are drawn on Hawthorne's forebears—the one "who lashed the Quaker woman so smartly through the streets" (stripped to the waist) and a leader of an Indian massacre "in King Phillip's war." The Devil says to Young Goodman Brown, "They were my good friends, both." Here is the Hawthorne smile again, and this time it is "the smile of welcome." Brown sees "the whole earth one stain of guilt, one mighty blood spot," so that "Evil is the nature of mankind." A key to the atrocities is that evil *is* pathological sexuality, the Devil's most convenient and darkest charge. One prays in church Sunday morning, but on Saturday night one dances naked in the moonlight.

The governess thinks like that. She is inspired by "Mrs. Rowson's famous tale," and she has just been reading, before the ghosts appear, *Amelia*, the story of a good woman leading her little boy and his younger sister through all the vices we find in *The Turn of the Screw* (the governess's parson father banned all novels at home). The sentimental conventions are observed; for example, if seduced, the poor woman pays with her life, usually in childbirth (or becomes a figure of living death, a streetwalker). One critic tells us that "Miss Jessel committed suicide"; another contends that she dies in childbirth (the critic sees a suggestion of pregnancy in Mrs. Grose's testimony, "she was not taken ill, *so far as appeared,* in this house"). Critics debate Peter Quint's death, too—maybe he was drunk, fell, and died from a blow to the head, or maybe he was murdered. The story is full of Gothic alternatives. And leaving matters open and vague like this was James's deliberate aim: "This, then, was the *amusette:* to terrify each reader with the fruits of his own imagination." "Only make the reader's general vision of evil intense enough, and his own experience, his own imagination, his own sympathy with the children and horror of their false friends will supply him quite sufficiently with all the particulars. Make him *think* the evil, make him think it for himself, and you are released from weak specifications." Those last two words remind me of that great James phrase I quoted earlier, "solidity of specification." In this preface James goes on to say that the ghosts should do only "as little as is consistent with their consenting to appear at all." No clanking chains or howls in the night. Quint appears in twilight, not a thunderstorm. When the governess sees Quint, "all the rest of the scene" seems to her "stricken with death" and an "intense hush" comes over it so that "all its voice" is lost and the rooks stop their cawing. Similarly with Miss Jessel; watching Flora, the governess says, "I was determined by a sense that within a minute all spontaneous sounds from her had dropped." James asks us to fill in those silences with our own specifications.

It has been argued that Miss Jessel and Peter Quint are not really ghosts at all; no, they are good fairies. Their business is to protect the children from the evil figures in the real world—the original parents who went off to India, the uncle who wants no word whatsoever about them (poor Mrs. Grose is right when she says, "He ought to *be* here—he ought to help"), the headmaster who expels Miles for "saying things." The governess is not set off to madness by nothing; if she finally comes to madness, it is through her passionate response to deep trouble in the real world.

My central objection to the Freudians is that they tend to make the governess trivial and ridiculous. I see her as a tragic figure, not a pathological case. Edna Kenton pointed out long ago that in James's "book of golden rules, no character is worth doing unless it is worth loving." James himself said Balzac's great achievement was that "he knew his creations by loving them."

The governess is right when she feels the world has wronged the children and that they are in danger. As I claimed earlier, she doesn't "invent" the Quint–Jessel escapade. It happened. She doesn't "invent" her employer who is so irresponsible nor Mrs. Grose who isn't bright enough to help and always yields her authority to her "superiors." Indeed, the lesson of the story might be that the world is evil—and makes us evil, too. Flora got her horrible language from someone. Miles did, too; he was expelled from school for using words that somebody taught him—and maybe they were terms of endearment (he only said them "to those I liked"). Affection was his crime. James wrote to a doctor friend of his, "the helpless plasticity of childhood that isn't dear or sacred to somebody! That was my little tragedy." And the only "somebody" who realizes the dear and the sacred in these children is the governess. It was inevitable, but unfortunate, that the critical discussion should largely divide readers into two armies, the apparitionists and the nonapparitionists, engaged in battle over the question of whether the ghosts are real or are in the governess's mind. The only adequate answer to that question is Yes.

The nonapparitionists humiliate the Governess. For example, "When Mrs. Grose asks what the apparition had to say, the governess promptly reports that Miss Jessel said that she was suffering the torments of the damned and has returned because she wants to 'share them' and 'wants Flora.' Actually, the only words spoken were the governess's shrieking at the intruder, 'You terrible, miserable woman!'" Note this critic's use of "actually." He *proves* the governess lies by checking her "story" against—her "story." Who knows?—maybe the first version was a lie! And, of course, the governess is always indicting herself, "I go on, I know, as if I were crazy."

Miles is constantly referred to as a little gentleman. But he's a *boy*. Elsewhere James remembers when he was forced, at age seven, to compose an apology for appearing barefoot at a seaside villa in front of guests. In the world of *The Turn of the Screw* Victorian chastity appears as prurience; sex is everywhere because it is denied everywhere—like those little white skirts on my grandmother's piano "limbs." As Stanley Renner has pointed out, the governess is "not really mad, merely deeply Victorian in the grip of a powerful cultural idea; she takes upon herself the role of angel in the house—guardian of idealized, spiritualized love and sexual purity." To which Mark Spilka adds "The young woman proceeds to fight the invading evil in the name of hothouse purity and domestic sainthood. That she destroys the children in saving them is understandable: her contemporaries were doing so all around her, and would do so for the next six decades." The governess lives in the romantic castle of Bly, the Victorian fantasy, besieged by sex ghosts in the Victorian nightmare. In the prologue to the tale a woman asks, "And what did the former governess die of?— so much respectability?" Exactly. With no experience, no training, the governess is charged with a huge responsibility, and she cracks—but she cracks under pressure that might crack us all. To understand the individual insanity you must consider very carefully the general madness. The world is full of ghosts: sinister presences are knocking on our windows, and they may get us. "Sex repression" isn't sexy. It's flat. It leaves out the world. In what way is this single governess's mind a part of the Victorian mind as well?

Children know more than they can deal with. Miles and Flora (and little Pearl in *The Scarlet Letter*) have extraordinary ESP. The governess finds Miles "as appealing as some wistful patient in a children's hospital," and Miles knows: he is acutely embarrassed by her feelings. He resents the way she hugs him to her; he knows something sinister is going on. These children are very suspicious angels. Somehow they *know.*

It is no accident that the great figures in horror stories include *Baron* von Frankenstein and *Count* Dracula. Their histories are available to us through "popular legend" and "folk superstitions." Our point of access to their horrible cruelty is told to us by the villagers, who know that the monster on the hill is the one who makes them live in cramped, cold misery. Surely the Evil One's amorous adventures involve sadism. This social

dimension to the story is before us constantly in the form of the governess's unsure status, at the bottom of the gentility and top of the hired
help. Her predecessor suffered "abasement." Violation of the body and violation of social status go together—as they do in *Lady Chatterly's Lover*—
when Quint, the "actor," violates the master's wardrobe and freely se-
duces the women on the staff. It is a conflation of sexual and social
indecencies. The governess, hearing of it for the first time, listens carefully
to Mrs. Grose's emphasis, "*She* was a lady," "And he was so dreadfully below." The Governess is a reliable Victorian girl.

Shoshana Felman says *The Turn of the Screw* is a familiar tale, a mystery
novel or detective story about the murder of a child: "As in all detective
stories, the crime is not uncovered until the end. But in contrast to the
classic mystery novel plot, this crime is also not committed until the end:
paradoxically enough, the process of detection here precedes the com-
mitting of the crime." Ms. Felman compares it to *Oedipus:* "The self-
proclaimed detective ends up discovering that he himself is the author of
the crime he is investigating." The story has the classical neatness of
tragedy. Richard Chase reminds us that

> a careful reading of the tale convinces us that the ghosts may really be
> there, marvellously adapted to but finally independent of the governess's
> fantasies. The governess is not a lunatic. Her version of reality is only in
> degree different from the false but precious and jealously guarded ver-
> sion we all form in our minds. In its desperate sensibility and intense cul-
> tivation it is particularly like the imagination of Henry James.

The governess's great duty is to protect the children from evil, and she
commits precisely the crime she wanted to prevent. But that does not
make her unreliable—save in the sense that we all are.

Chapter Nine

What Maisie Saw

F.W. Dupee observes that "it is not unusual in James for the overtones of one novel to become the themes of the next." He notes that Mrs. Wix in *What Maisie Knew* is "almost diabolical" in her effort to protect her charge from the sinister forces around her; we lose the "almost" when Mrs. Wix becomes, in the following year, the governess. Both books present "a strange medium of exasperated curiosity" which explores "unknowable sexual relations."

In his notebook on December 22, 1895, James wrote, "It takes place before Maisie—EVERYTHING TAKES PLACE BEFORE MAISIE." The wonderful 1913 Sargent portrait of Henry James at seventy (in which James saw himself as "all large and luscious rotundity") was, while on exhibition the following year in the Royal Academy, slashed by a suffragette. The Penguin edition of *Maisie* uses as "cover art" a detail from Sargent's masterpiece, "The Daughters of Edward D. Boit"—the little girl, with that great gorgeous vase behind her, does indeed look like our Maisie. And we can see Maisie, exactly, and her predicament, exactly, in a *New Yorker* cartoon. It shows a cocktail party, and the little girl (seven years old? eight?) is serving hors d'oeuvres. She stands with her tray before a seated lady who asks her—the caption could be the epigraph to the novel—"And whose little marriage are we?"

John Singer Sargent, "The Daughters of Edward Darley Boit."
Gift of Mary Louisa Boit, Julia Overing Boit, Jane Hubbard Boit,
and Florence D. Boit in memory of their father, Edward Darley Boit.
Courtesy, Museum of Fine Arts, Boston.

In calling this chapter "What Maisie Saw," I am trying to locate and emphasize something that James already expresses in his notebook. Any card-carrying Jacobite will recognize the phrases, but in this case they appear with a special, almost obsessive urgency: "Voyons un peu . . . Voyons, Voyons . . . voyons . . . Yes, I see. . . . Voyons, voyons . . . I seem to see this. . . . I see Mrs. W. 'come down';—I see Mrs. Beale 'come down';—I see Mrs. W. come down again. . . . the scenic method is my absolute, my imperative, my only salvation."

This concern with seeing and looking continues in the prose of the novel itself, from that famous opening description, "her little world was phantasmagoric—strange shadows dancing on a sheet," to the invigoration of cliché in "you'll see for yourself," and even to Maisie's marvelous little error, calling Gower Street "Glower Street." "She went about as sightlessly as if he had been leading her blindfold" and "so conscious of being more frightened than she had ever been in her life . . . she seemed to see her whiteness as in a glass."

That last figure again reminds us that this imagery is not a radical departure; for Isabel Archer saw her problem "as distinctly as if it had been reflected in a large clear glass." Indeed, the magnificent chapter 42 of *The Portrait of a Lady* is itself "pure seeing," "the vigil of searching criticism." Isabel ponders that "remembered vision" of her husband and Mme. Merle "familiarly associated." Isabel, "her mind assailed by visions," scans "the future with dry, fixed eyes." The very title of the book asks us to see.

What appears only briefly in the *Portrait* is Isabel's sense that her husband has "the evil eye." The year following *Maisie*, in *The Turn of the Screw*, Peter Quint has "the evil eye." This story is an "excursion into chaos," and the governess, constantly worrying that she has an "insane look," sees her own crazy eyes in those of others—"Do I look very queer?" "I looked prodigious things." Mrs. Grose speaks of Miss Jessel's "awful eyes," and then "stared at mine as if they might really have resembled them." People look queer, look ugly; indeed, the whole tale comes out of the governess's evil eye, for the meaning she sees in the world destroys—she kills her charge with her vision. Hester Prynne knew, ages before, what it was like, the paralysis of being seen, standing in shame, being stared at. And we've all said, "What are you looking at?" We remember it from childhood—"Make him stop looking at me." Maisie is pierced, straight through, by all the awful looks thrust upon her, and she, in turn, also looks: "There was literally an instant in which Maisie saw—saw madness and desolation, saw ruin and darkness and death."

Of course, you could say I'm making it too dark. James himself called *Maisie* "an ugly little comedy." Wit and gusto are everywhere. It's fun, real fun, when Maisie notices the way Sir Claude watches the bathing beauties: he "followed the fine stride and shining limbs of a young fishwife who had just waded out of the sea with her basketful of shrimps. His thought came back to her sooner than his eyes." We can hardly resist Mrs. Beale's delicious characterization of Mrs. Wix: "she drivels when she doesn't rage." My own favorite line is about Maisie's mother: she had a "bosom cut remarkably low. She was always in a fearful hurry, and the lower the bosom was cut the more it was to be gathered she was wanted elsewhere."

But this comedy moves swiftly from the robust to the raw, from high spirits to genuine pain. "Her father called her a dirty little donkey" is surely one of the nastiest lines in all of James. "He lighted a cigarette and began to smoke in her face." There is real shock here, and we're on to it from the very beginning where Maisie is described as "a ready vessel for their bitterness, a deep little porcelain cup in which biting acids could be mixed." The characters speak extravagantly; their hyperbole, which at first looks like comic overstatement, eventually involves the truly terrible: "she has chucked our friend here overboard not a bit less than if she had shoved her, shrieking and pleading, out of that window and down two floors to the paving-stones" (an image that is picked up a year later for little Miles: "he uttered the cry of a creature hurled over an abyss"). It's funny that "Mrs. Wix gave the jerk a sleeper awakened or the start even of one who hears a bullet whiz at the flag of truce"—very funny, yes, but also extremely unsettling.

This is the language of violence. The figures of speech do not so much enrich the prose as they violate it, shake it dreadfully, startling its assurance of tone. We feel the violence even in James's own voice, in his prefatory remark about his theme: "Once out, like a housedog of a temper above confinement, it defies the mere whistle, it roams, it hunts, it seeks out and "sees" life; it can be brought back but by hand and then only to take its futile thrashing." Notice that he puts 'sees' in quotation marks, and notice especially how imaginative activity must be punished, even in a housedog. Maisie's mother, billiards champ extraordinaire, is perhaps the most physically violent creature in the whole Jamesian menagerie. She receives pretty stiff competition, however, from Mrs. Wix, the governess in this book, and the governess of *The Turn of the Screw*; both of these "caregivers," full of suppressed howls, clutch and grab and pull and yank and smother and crush their charges to their breasts. All the pummeling fosters a grossly premature senility, oddly witchlike: the governess says of Flora, "she's not a child; she's an old, old woman," and Sir Claude says to Maisie, "I'm always talking to you in the most extraordinary way, ain't I? One would think you were about sixty."

I should like to turn from the purely visual (seeing) to the largely artistic (painting). In his preface to *Maisie* James says that the initial subject "gave out that vague pictorial glow which forms the first appeal of a living 'subject' to the painter's consciousness." When our heroine is whisked off to France, "her vocation was to see the world and to thrill with enjoyment of the picture . . . the place and the people were all a picture together, a picture that, when they went down to the wide sands, shimmered, in a thousand tints, with the pretty organization of the *plage* [beach]." A half-dozen years later James locates Lambert Strether in the same terms, in the French countryside, where the landscape "fell into a composition, full of felicity . . . the sky was silver and turquoise and varnish; the village on the left was white and the church on the right was grey; it was all there, in short—it was Tremont Street, it was France, it was Lambinet. Moreover, he was freely walking about in it." Both the pubescent girl and the elderly bachelor see life as an Impressionist landscape painting. Miraculously, they walk right into it.

Read around in *The Ambassadors* for ten pages anywhere, substituting "I" for "he." You don't have to change anything else (there is no scene where Strether isn't present). You'll find that the result is rather astonishing, even eerie. I think I am saying something more than, or at least something different from, the classic defense of Percy Lubbock. The crucial definition of point of view, which saves James's books from the bin of "baggy monsters," provides expressive means to render dramatically what might seem flat as mere first-person narrative. To be sure, that is true. But I mean something else. When I performed my trick of "I" rather than "he," I discovered that the pronoun changes whatever is there, whether vivid or flat, because it changes profoundly who Strether is. If "he" is "I," Strether isn't nearly as funny. He's downright creepy. He's terribly self-important. He's Miles Coverdale.

Lambert Strether suffers from what today some might call "blockage." He can't articulate what he doesn't know; Strether's ignorance is not something he can talk about with himself. Strether's not knowing is by definition his central flaw, or failure, or problem: he's forever being blind-sided. The job is not really to vivify what is known, as Lubbock would have it, but to make intrinsic, as a subject of rich interest, the failures of knowing. "I" just makes Strether our old friend the unreliable narrator. That is most Jamesian, of course (consider *The Turn of the Screw*, or what seems to me the masterpiece of this mode, *The Aspern Papers*). But to do it with our chief emissary from Woollett is to compromise his imaginative appeal. "He" is a "dear man." "I" isn't dear. "He lay on his back on the grass" won't work when we substitute "I" because we would feel the grass on our back instead of seeing the man himself lying in the grass. If "I" "pulled my straw hat over my eyes" the lights would go out. We can't *see*. "I" ruins the fun in "he went down to Rouen with a little handbag and inordinately spent the night." That supremely mischievous adverb, "inordinately," would be funked if "I" were consciously to say it. The wrong perspective before our eyes is the wrong voice in our ears.

For me one of the very strongest and most touching lines of the entire novel would be absolutely inconceivable—clammy—if Strether had *told* us about it: "he almost blushed, in the dark, for the way he had dressed the possibility in vagueness, as a little girl might have dressed her doll." The narrative gives out a grand little moan—grand because the character cannot himself put it into words. If he could tell us, it would make him merely precious.

My point here is that something of the same thing, with the same effect, goes on in *What Maisie Knew*. It is the opposite of what one might expect—the intimacy is deeper, closer, with "she" instead of "I." Or, we might call it an emotional synesthesia, the simultaneous sense of intimacy and distance. Where indeed are we in the following two sentences?—

"Maisie could only have a sense of something that in a maturer mind would be called the way history repeats itself" and "Maisie looked at Mrs. Cuddon hard—her lips even echoed the name." Maisie doesn't have the maturer mind; Maisie doesn't realize that her lips echo the name. We have the remarkable sensation of being the girl at the same time that we are watching her. Reading, we become, with a wince, *self-conscious.*

Look at how it would all go wrong if Maisie herself were to say "*I* was awestruck at the manner in which a lady might be affected through the passion mentioned by Mrs. Wix." Or: "This was a course our delicacy shrank from." Sir Claude says, "If you'll help me, you know, I'll help you." How dreadful—how prurient—"she" would be if "it gave *me* moments of secret rapture—moments of believing I might help him indeed." The innocence is soiled.

But then, of course, the soiling of innocence is what the novel is all about. As our heroine "grows," as she "develops," as what she knows becomes richer and deeper, we watch with dismay, our hearts sinking. Perhaps "dismay" is not strong enough, insufficiently urgent—better to say "alarm," for Maisie is getting good at a game she should never have to play. She is learning all sorts of deeply troubling things about sex and love and power, sinister things about taking pleasure in doing harm. The only emotion you can finally count on is self-interest. To tell that story in her own voice, Maisie would have to take command. And which would compel the slower, graver shake of our head?—that she "got it," or that she got it wrong? The child is utterly without playmates, without any experience of other children her own age. She must move in a world of adults; even when she thinks they love her, they call her a "poor little monkey." And she comes to think that that is what she is.

In the very last lines of the book, on the boat, Mrs. Wix says to her:

"I didn't look back, did you?"

"Yes. He wasn't there," said Maisie.

"Not on the balcony?"

Maisie waited a moment; then "He wasn't there," she simply said again.

Mrs. Wix was also silent a while. "He went to her," she finally observed.

"Oh I know!" the child replied.

Mrs. Wix gave a sidelong look. She still had room for wonder at what Maisie knew.

Note all the looking—looking back, looking sidelong. Note, too, that "I" can't "say simply." It must be "the child's" reply, for we realize that she isn't, really, a child anymore. Indeed, I would note finally that the hushed pain, the death of childhood, comes, like a physical blow, from the terrific disappointment of what Maisie *didn't* see.

Chapter Ten

"The Americana"

In 1880 Henry James wrote to his friend Thomas Sergeant Perry (who was prepared to write an omnibus review of all James's work so far), "I would rather you should wait a few months, til my *big* novel (to be published this year) comes out. It is from that I shall myself pretend to date—on that I shall take my stand." *"Big" The Portrait of a Lady* would become, twice as long as anything he had previously written, and *"big"* because it is the first major work to prove him a genius.

I often begin classroom discussion of the book by having the students read and commit to memory the first sentence: "Under certain circumstances, there are few hours in life more agreeable than the hour dedicated to the ceremony known as afternoon tea." When I challenge anyone to quote the sentence word perfect, the usual mistakes include "hours in the day" and "pleasurable" for "hour in life" and "agreeable." I ask the class, "How old is the speaker?" "Is he American or British?" "Is it a comic voice or a tragic voice?" I confess I think the first page of the novel is the most perfect first page in our literature. The students call it "witty," but I caution them that it's clearly not witty in the manner of Oscar Wilde—there are no aphorisms, no epigrams, no particularly quotable lines. The pace is supremely assured. Twenty-five years later, James made several big changes on the closing pages, his description of Isabel's first and only kiss, but in the beginning, on the first page, he changed not a word.

Henry James and Cora Taylor ("Mrs. Stephen Crane").
Courtesty, Rare Book and Manuscript Library, Columbia University.

For its tone alone the page is remarkable; it conveys ease, warmth, great good humor. It is mock heroic in the conversation of three gentlemen taking their tea: they make mountains out of molehills; the smaller the molehill, the bigger the mountain. The appeal is to intelligence, leisure, clear seeing, grace. It is Olympian fun; Lord Warburton was sick only once, "in the Persian Gulf." This is true freedom. As Richard Poirier has pointed out, there is an "elegant prissiness" about it: the speaker is indeed American, but he has defected to "the other side." It is a voice of pure joy and careful mischief.

The working title had been "The Americana." Tony Tanner makes a nice British error when he says that Isabel Archer comes from "Albany, New England." Sure she does. Old Mrs. Touchett provides comic relief to the grim experience of the final chapters; when she hears Madame Merle has been exiled to her native land, "Crazy Aunt Lydia" says, "To America? She must have done something very bad." James wrote in the last paragraph of his preface to the New York edition that his job in "treating" his story included "never forgetting, by any lapse, that the thing was under special obligation to be amusing." One of the clearest instances of that is Henrietta, the young lady who bears the feminine form of her author's own first name; it is Miss Stackpole who is "the Americana," the one who looks out on the world with a transparent eyeball—James refers frequently to her "peculiarly open, surprised looking eye," eyes that remind Ralph "of large polished buttons," eyes "lighted like great glazed railway stations." Only an "Americana" could make Henrietta's wonderful conflation: "I should like so much to visit the sights with you, I wish to see as much as possible of the inner life." She is very funny, of course, but she has a generous, good heart; she crosses the Atlantic in midwinter "because she had guessed Isabel was sad." As Ralph would say, if you need a friend, Henrietta's your man!

Poirier notes that Henrietta "is the kind of character who believes certain things which James admires but who does so in a foolishly compulsive way." Henrietta, Poirier says, "draws off the poison, as it were. The author knows how silly the matter *can* be, and it therefore leaves him free to be as serious about it as he chooses." James is as playful about Henrietta as his characters are with each other. When Ralph says to his father, Lord Warburton is "making light of you, daddy," James joins his voice with Ralph's, quoting what "daddy replied." James clearly enjoys giving Isabel lines like "Oh, I hoped there would be a lord; it's just like a novel!" and "I adore a moat." James tells us about Isabel's sense of the word "wicked"— "She knew the idea only by the Bible and other literary works." Note that delicious "other."

My students sometimes fail to realize that James knows perfectly well what's wrong with Isabel; in the first hundred pages he keeps telling us, almost to redundancy. Through that voice of his we—with him—expect to see her taken down a peg:

> She often wondered indeed if she ever had been, or even could be, intimate with anyone.

> She was too young, too impatient to live, too unacquainted with pain.

> It may be affirmed without delay that Isabel was probably very liable to the sin of self-esteem.

> It was of no use, she had an unquenchable desire to think well of herself.

> Sometimes she went so far as to wish that she might find herself some day in a difficult position, so that she should have the pleasure of being as heroic as the occasion demanded.

We read these passages silently saying to her, Be careful what you wish for, young lady, because you might just get it. James concludes these admonitions with a caution flag: "she would be an easy victim of scientific criticism if she were not intended to awaken on the reader's part an impulse more tender and more purely expectant."

Some of the young men in my classes, especially the athletes, refuse to be "purely expectant" because they sense Isabel wouldn't go for them, and they know why, dammit; the girl's "frigid." They point to how often James emphasizes it:

> "I'm afraid," said Isabel. After a pause she repeated as if to make herself, rather than Ralph, hear the words. "I'm afraid."

"I always come back to myself. It's because I'm afraid." She stopped; her voice had trembled a little. "Yes, I'm afraid."

She was afraid of her visitor and she was ashamed of her fear.

Twice she says directly, to Lord Warburton, "I'm afraid of you," and twice when Caspar Goodwood leaves her, "she burst into tears." The companion emotion to gaiety is Gothic; as Joseph Wiesenfarth says, Isabel's mind, her language, her metaphors are full of cages, prisons, dungeons, torture, evil eyes, serpents, demons, poison, mold and decay. Anthony J. Mazella insists, over and over, "She is not afraid merely of the erotic experience itself but rather its tendency to diminish the life of the mind"; her fear is "the annihilation of the mind by the erotic"; she fears "control by the erotic of the mind's power to operate," and "the erotic is a threat to the mind's activity." Professor Mazella has, it seems to me, rather too literally taken to heart the admonition to "fuck your brains out." Isabel tries to tell herself that Warburton's passion "had sifted itself clear to the baser parts of emotion—the heat, the violence, the unreason—and that burned as steadily as a lamp in a windless place." She is genuinely and deeply afraid of Caspar; what's wrong with him is his sexual aggressiveness: "there was a disagreeably strong push, a kind of hardness of presence, in his way of rising before her." To interpret this in Freudian terms might seem specious if there were only one sexual pun, but it seems unavoidable when you consider all three.

I am always amazed by what critics make of these matters. Alfred Habegger, for example, scrutinizes the Touchett men, father and son, and says that "what we are dealing with here is James's unconscious projection onto Ralph, with James exposing more than he intended of the obligatory or slavish aspect of his relationship with his father. Mr. Touchett's bank corresponds to Henry Sr.'s philosophy." That word "corresponds" stops me in my tracks, and I always have trouble with critics who point to anything in James that is "an unconscious projection" or his stupid habit of "exposing more than he had intended." Neither relationship—James to his father or Ralph to his—strikes me as "slavish." But Habegger has bigger fish to fry: Isabel's "empowerment" derives from Dan Touchett's "extinction, and the vital transfer has been engineered by none other than the supposedly loyal son. This is why Ralph must die: he has recklessly handed over the patriarch's vital stuff to a girl who cannot help squandering it, and the fathers are not to be appeased." Comparing Ralph and Dan to Pansy and her father, Habegger concludes that "if we ask what kind of novelist could possibly ask us to accept this idyllic father–son bond, the answer is irresistible: He must have been a Pansy." (If we are to think of "Pansy" only as the girl's name, not homophobic slang, a few lines later Habegger writes "*The Portrait* is the artifact of a brilliant but uneasy pansy." Small p.)

Other critics, while not as obscenely vicious, are equally absurd. To my class I cited one who proposes that "imperialism is a major issue in *The Portrait of a Lady,* and Osmond is 'the Disraeli' of the book." The class laughed, harder than I expected, but the vehemence of their guffaw pleased me (until in office hours a student said he thought it was so funny that anybody could think Osmond was an "Israeli"). But what is one to make of Sheldon M. Novick's claim in *Henry James, the Young Master* (1996) that James "performed his first acts of love" on Oliver Wendell Holmes, Jr.? Novick says, "the passage is impossible to misunderstand." No, Millicent Bell, in her review of Mr. Novick's book (*TLS,* December 6, 1996), says James was talking not at all about sexual initiation; rather, it was a "*literary* initiation" (her italics); James was referring to his decision to quit law school and become a full-time writer. Novick says it is "startling and funny" that James refers to his seeing "the Bunker Hill obelisk point as sharply as ever its beveled capstone against the sky." Novick calls this phallic image "discreet" but "unmistakable." The only problem is that it's a quotation from Holmes, Sr., expressing his profound relief on his son's safe return from the Civil War.

Novick proposes that in England Henry James "could bury his nose in the sleeve of a new woolen coat and enjoy the scent." Now how would Novick know that? Nowhere does James say that about himself. Bell rightly complains that Novick slips in and out of Jamesian prose, frequently without indicating so with quotation marks. In this matter of burying a nose in the sleeve to scent the wool, Novick is stealing James's description in *Portrait* of Madame Merle who "used to lift the sleeve of her British overcoat and bury her nose in it, inhaling the clear, fine scent of the wool." Which is why, I guess, that Novick says, "Costumed as

Madame Merle, James performed his greatest impersonation." Novick's professed modesty is a red flag: "I have not made any special discoveries about James's sexuality; James's sexual orientation, as we now say, has been an open secret for a hundred years." Not open to me, and certainly not what Novick describes as "a rather old-fashioned, Freudian view of 'homosexuality' as a kind of failure."

But Novick doesn't sink his fingers into nothing. *The New York Times* (in a review of the recent movie of *Portrait*) is correct to say that "the resurgence of interest in James has coincided with the rise of 'gay' and 'gender' studies, and many contemporary scholars read James's novels as disguised homosexual love stories." I have read and heard frequent claims that Ralph is a disguised homosexual. Old Dan Touchett says he thinks his son is in love with Isabel. Ralph replies, "No, I'm not in love with her; but I should be—if certain things were different." Gay scholars tell me, "There it is!—'if certain things were different' means 'if I were not a homosexual.'" I answer back, "But no, right there in the text itself we have it—'different' means, 'if she weren't my cousin and if I weren't dying of tuberculosis'; "people in an advanced stage of pulmonary disorder shouldn't marry at all." But, oh no, comes the reply, "Surely you can see through *that*. In 1880—and in 1908, too—James couldn't afford to be explicit; it is a sign of the times that a gay character had to have a 'cover disease.' Besides, if you insist on a literal reading of the text, the old man says "We're all each other's cousins, and if we stopped at that the human race would die out."

I hope I am not guilty of "unconscious projection" or "exposing more than I intend" when I insist on a question: what does it say about Dan Touchett if he doesn't know his son is gay? I think of an obtuse colleague of mine who said to his handsome teen age son, "Tell me anything—just don't tell me you're a queer." But the son *was* Queer, and if Dan Touchett doesn't know his son's affectional preference, then he is an old fool. But he is not an old fool. He's the wisest man in the book (or his son is). James tells us early on that Ralph thinks of his father "as his best friend." In one of their last conversations, Dan asks, "Why should we prevaricate just at the last? We never prevaricated before." If my opponents are correct, father and son have prevaricated for many, many years. It's all prevarication.

I think it throws the entire novel out of joint, all the way to Ralph's deathbed and beyond. Look carefully at the sentence "The old man lay there looking at his son; his face was the face of the dying, but his eyes were the eyes of Daniel Touchett." It is extraordinary, as you can see if you substitute your own father's name (if you love/d him) for "Daniel Touchett." Ralph is the conscience of the book, and Ralph's father is Ralph's conscience. Ralph is making a major mistake in this scene, and his father points out to him his blunder:

> "It seems to me immoral."
> "Well, I don't know that it's right to make everything so easy for a person. Doesn't it occur to you that a young lady with sixty thousand pounds may fall victim to the fortune-hunters?"
> "She'll hardly fall victim to more than one."
> "Well one's too many."

The sixty thousand pounds becomes seventy (roughly two million dollars in today's money). It is a tremendous sum; Ralph "should like to make her rich," and when his father asks, "What do you mean by rich?," Ralph immediately answers with one of the most daring lines in the book, "I call people rich when they're able to meet the requirements of their imagination." At that his father groans, "Don't tell me you're not in love with her!"

If the old man's wrong, we have to read all the rest of the book as "code." I see no reason to do so, and several reasons not to. In the final scene between Isabel and Ralph, those great intimate exchanges between them, what if Ralph, drawing his last breaths, is still stuck in his closet? Is he lying when he "just audibly and lingeringly breathed, 'you've also been loved. Ah but, Isabel—*adored*!' " I certainly do not mean that a homosexual person is incapable of this speech, this deep feeling; I simply mean that to read everything looking for its "real" meaning diverts our attention from the developing narrative energy in those grand rooms and leads us to a futile search for "clues" in the closet. We pay attention to James's equivocating timidity, not to his power. Everything's a crossword puzzle.

For a rather different but still major error, there is Patricia Stubbs's study "Feminism and the Novel":

> In James we meet pure ideology and an anti-feminism so subtle and fused so completely with the form and texture of the novel it can be

overlooked altogether. James's artistic control is so complete that the reader is tricked into accepting the unacceptable. Isobel's marrying Osmond [Throughout, Stubbs misspells "Isabel" as "Isobel."] is left unmotivated—a curious omission for such a careful artist. He fails to justify the most important single event in the novel. If the decision is, as many critics suggest, out of character, then it must come directly from James himself. "Well done" though the book is, it is rooted in suspicion, and its resolution suggests a degree of hostility to the idea of real independence for women.

Can this argument be, by any stretch of the imagination, true? Why does Isabel make such a terrible mistake? When Osmond says to her, "I'm absolutely in love with you," we know that he's not. We know him rather well before she even meets him. We know he's an esthete from his "extremely modelled and composed face," his beard "cut in the manner of the portraits of the sixteenth century" (note "the portraits of," not the sixteenth century). He is "a gentleman who studied style," "fine gold coin as he was," "the elegant complicated medal struck off for a special occasion." That is, the first thing we know about him is that he's sinister, and we hear it in the nun's hesitation about Pansy, " 'She draws very—very carefully.' " We have heard Osmond say to Madame Merle, "I'm sick of my adorable taste," and that when he says of Ralph, "He's a good deal of a donkey," Madame Merle has to correct him, "I think you're mistaken. He's a very clever man." Isabel herself gets it exactly backward: "Ralph had something of this same quality, this appearance of thinking that life was a matter of connoisseurship; but in Ralph it was an anomaly, a kind of humorous excrescence, whereas in Mr. Osmond it was the keynote, and everything was in harmony with it." The truth is that Gilbert Osmond is *merely* "a student of the exquisite." He has no sense of humor. Ralph is always funny; Osmond, never. Humor is liberating; unrelieved solemnity is confining. The comic is essential to the moral sense, and Osmond "takes himself so seriously." His cruelty is unmistakable: "He found the silver quality in Isabel; he could tap her imagination with his knuckle and make it ring."

To return to Stubbs's objection, Isabel can't understand this because she has never been inside his head, and we have. Stubbs wonders why "Isobel" can't see through him, since everyone else does. James makes that dramatically clear: Isabel sees her friends' and relatives' disapproval as "the tragic part of happiness." She lives like the heroine of a novel, and she has learned from novels that "the passion of love separated its victim terribly from everyone but the loved object. She felt herself disjoined from everyone she had known before." Aunt Lydia disapproves, but, Isabel tells herself, look at Aunt Lydia's own marriage. With pert cruelty she sees Ralph's disapproval as "surely but a whimsical cover for a personal disappointment." That animosity "made him say angry things about the man she had preferred even to him." And Caspar—well, he never shuts up.

Even after Isabel has immersed herself fully in the shallows of Osmond's malicious spirit, she still tries to do her duty. Toward the end of the book Osmond comes out with what most critics treat as a thundering platitude, "What I value most in life is the honour of a thing." What status does such an utterance have in Isabel's mind? She thinks, "He spoke gravely and almost gently; the accent of sarcasm had dropped out of his tone. His words were not a command, they constituted a kind of appeal, they represented something transcendent and absolute, like the sign of the cross or the flag of one's country." "He was sincere" and that "was a merit," and she is struggling to be a good wife.

Most importantly, Isabel is completely under the spell of the woman who has arranged the marriage, Madame Merle. In her infatuation Isabel "wandered, as by the wrong side of the wall of a private garden, round the enclosed talents, accomplishments, aptitudes of Madame Merle. She found herself desiring to emulate them, and in twenty such ways this lady presented herself as a model. 'I should like awfully to be *so!*' Isabel secretly exclaimed, more than once, as one after another of her friend's fine aspects caught the light." Madame Merle "knew how to think" and "of course, too, she knew how to feel. This was indeed Madame Merle's great talent, her most perfect gift. Life had told upon her; she had felt it strongly." She is an example of James's best villianesses: they are sensual (always the most sexual character in every novel in which they make an appearance), and they have the knowledge that the heroines are seeking. In his Madame Merles, his Kate Croys, his Charlotte Stants, James is clearly obsessed with this sort of woman. Madame Merle's great speech about "What shall we call our 'self'? Where does it begin, where does it end?," announces in true Jamesian fashion, "I've a great respect for *things!*" When Isabel disagrees, "My clothes may express the dressmaker, but they don't express me," Madame Merle wins, firing a single sexual bullet, "Should you prefer to go without them?"

The one time Madame Merle drops her guard, Isabel is not there. "Madame Merle was seldom guilty of the awkwardness of retracting what she had said," but she fails to express sympathy for Mrs. Touchett after Dan's death; crudely Madame Merle enunciates an awful adjective: "Am I not to see your happy niece?"

Meanwhile, Isabel is hopelessly lost in her own novel. Henrietta says to her, "You think you can lead a romantic life, but you're mistaken," and "from the moment you do that it ceases to be romance, I assure you: it becomes grim reality." Isabel still thinks "a swift carriage, of a dark night, rattling with four horses over roads that one can't see—that's my idea of happiness." Henrietta properly observes, "Mr. Goodwood certainly didn't teach you to say such things as that." Henrietta accuses her friend of aspiring to be "the heroine of an immoral novel," and warns "You're drifting to some great mistake."

She is. Her marrying Osmond is entirely in character. She says, so proud of her choice, "Give me up, Mr. Goodwood, I'm marrying a perfect nonentity." It surely prepares us for her realization, too late—and what a tremendous blow, what a terrific injury to her opinion of herself it is—that she made a colossal blunder. Warnings were everywhere; she missed each and every one of them. She must live the rest of her life increasingly aware of her abject failure at the most important job she would ever have to do.

I have a long-standing debate with my colleague Jonathan Bishop that to this day we still enjoy. Jonathan sees a flaw in the book's plot. In chapter 35's penultimate paragraph Amy Gemini speaks of her mother as "the American Corinne" (James's little joke about Margaret Fuller, who was known as "the American Corinne"). The next chapter begins with what could be the first sentence of a novel:

One afternoon of the autumn of 1876, toward dusk, a young man of pleasing appearance rang at the door of a small apartment of the third floor of an old Roman house.

As we read it, if we have paid attention, we realize that a few years—about three?—have passed. James said to a young writer, "I find that the very most difficult thing in the art of the novelist is to give the impression of the *real lapse of time, the quantity* of time" (his italics). The "lapse" here is notable by its absence. We wonder what has happened to Isabel; given our knowledge of what a monster Osmond is, we want to know what he has done to our Isabel—has Osmond changed her? How? We do not get any immediate answers to those questions. A few pages later, Madame Merle tells us, through young Rosier, that Isabel "had a poor little boy, who died two years ago, six months after his birth." And in chapter 39, James tells us, through Ralph, "She had lost her child; that was a sorrow, but it was a sorrow she scarcely spoke of; there was more to say about it than she could say to Ralph. It belonged to the past, moreover; it had occurred six months before, and she had already laid aside the tokens of mourning." That is all we hear about the lost child. It curiously doesn't seem to have registered.

Jonathan said to me that James lets us down by refusing to tell us a fascinating story—Isabel's pregnancy, the death of the child, and the discovery of Osmond's true nature. It could be of rich interest, and James leaves it almost a complete blank. Some critics say the child's brief appearance is James's telegraphic assurance that Isabel and Osmond actually slept together. In light of what I have said above about Isabel's timorous sexuality—her fear of Warburton and especially Caspar Goodwood—we should notice that Osmond presented no such threat. He seemed entirely passive, devoid of sexual passion. Isabel felt in him "only the nobleness and purity." Countess Gemini is correct: Isabel has "a beastly pure mind." The baby's birth shows that Isabel and Osmond are at least "normal," sexually, and the baby's death is "normal," too, in a time when infant mortality rates were so high.

But I have not yet answered Jonathan's objection, and I should like to try. James postpones, for quite some time, our understanding of the changed Isabel. First he gives us all the Rosier–Pansy material, which is interesting enough, but we don't really know what has become of our heroine. When she says of Osmond, "He has a genius for upholstery," that at least tells us a little. But we look at her in roughly the same way Ralph does:

There was something fixed and mechanical in the serenity painted on her face; this was not an expression, Ralph said, it was a representation, it was even an advertisement. There was a kind of violence in some of her impulses, of crudity in some of her experiments, which took him by surprise; it seemed to him that she even spoke faster, moved faster than before her marriage. Certainly she had fallen into exaggerations—she who used to care so much for the pure truth; of old she had a great delight in good-humoured argument, in intellectual play (she never looked so charming as when in the genial heat of discussion she received a crushing blow full in the face and brushed it away as a feather).

The ground under our feet has shifted. "The free, keen girl had become quite another person." Now "her light step drew a mass of drapery behind it; her intelligent head sustained a majesty of ornament"; now she is a "fine lady"—which suddenly brings the title of the book into question. Straight step-by-step narrative, by definition, could not provide us with this mystery. We are already waiting for chapter 42, even though we don't know it exists. What we do know is that we need to see her; rather, whatever has happened to her, we want to know what she has learned and how she has been changed by it. So far her "look" has been "inscrutable."

One thing for which I cannot forgive Isabel is her response to Ralph's declaration, "I've said what I had on my mind—and I've said it because I love you." At that, "Isabel turned pale; was he too on that tiresome list? She had a sudden wish to strike him off." That's how our girl thinks before her marriage; her self-infatuation and unconscious cruelty come as a kind of blow. Now, after the marriage, the birth and death of a baby, after joy and sorrow, after clear disappointment, we want to know if she still thinks in such vain and ugly terms.

The answer begins with a discovered intimacy, something like what happens in *The Ambassadors* when Strether catches sight of a little boat in which Chad and Madame de Vionnet sit. Here it is an "impression"— James henceforth uses that word abundantly—when Isabel discovers Osmond seated and Madame Merle standing. "There was an anomaly in this that arrested her." She "perceived that they had arrived at a desultory pause in their exchange of ideas and were musing, face to face, with the freedom of old friends who sometimes exchange ideas without uttering them. There was nothing to shock in this; they were old friends in fact. But the thing made an image, lasting only a moment, like a sudden flicker of light." The always poised Madame Merle "welcomed her without moving. Her husband, on the other hand, had instantly jumped up," and by so doing he has stupidly provided Isabel with the ability to discover that "the cup of experience" is, indeed, "a poisoned drink."

James called chapter 42 "obviously the best thing in the book," and added that "it is only a supreme illustration of the general plan." He is talking about "the long statement, just beyond the middle of the book, of my young woman's extraordinary meditative vigil on the occasion that was to become for her such a landmark. Reduced to its essence, it is but the vigil of searching criticism; but it throws the action further forward than twenty 'incidents' might have done. It was designed to have all the vivacity of incident and all the economy of picture." It is "a representation simply of her motionless seeing," and it is "as 'interesting' as the surprise of a caravan or the identification of a pirate." "It all goes on without her being approached by another person, and without her leaving her chair." That is, chapter 42 is pure sensibility, pure rumination, a portrait of the soul in action. The most interesting thing in a James novel is for someone to think.

The book was written on trains and in train stations, various hotel rooms and apartments, on boats and in villas, written in England, Italy, France, and Scotland. Yet *Portrait* displays an astonishing consistency of tone. For a book already being published serially before James had finished it, the plot is entirely consistent. When we read chapter 42 I ask my students to keep an early scene in mind, where Ralph anticipates in many ways what Isabel does here. In chapter 15 of volume 1, Ralph went home at night to an empty house. He took up a candle, and "the square was still; when he raised one of the windows of the dining-room to let in the air he heard the slow creak of the boots of a lone constable" (one of the finest, most memorable *sounds* in the book because it keys the emotion). "Ralph sat down in one of the arm-chairs" and "the big dark dining table twinkled here and there in the small candle light." James tells us that Ralph's "imagination took flight," and "he remained in his chair a long time beyond the hour at which he should have been in bed; doing nothing, not even reading the evening paper." He was thinking of Isabel.

Notice how chapter 42 repeats, in the same details and in general feeling, Ralph's "meditative vigil"—the candle, the lateness of the hour, the solitary concentration. It is as much praying as thinking. Isabel has a big decision to make, and goes right to work on it: if Warburton "was in love with Pansy he was not in love with her stepmother, and if he was in love with her stepmother he was not in love with Pansy. Was she to cultivate the advantage she possessed in order to make him commit himself to Pansy, knowing he would do so for her and not for the small creature's own—was this the service her husband asked of her?" She has realized that "she should play the part of a good wife. She wanted to be that; she wanted to be able to believe sincerely, and with proof of it, she had been that." She felt that she was "trying as much as possible to take her husband's view." But now, the first thing she thinks of during her vigil, is that "it was not an agreeable task; it was in fact a repulsive one."

She had wanted her life to be a novel. Well, now it is—an old novel, a bad novel. But she is by no means a pathetic victim. Her spiritual journey gathers together all the key images in the book—the gardens, the flowers there, the houses, the wings, the eyes (both evil and benign). Importantly, this is the way she thinks—the chapter we have been waiting for—the Jamesian narrator has quite disappeared, no longer hanging around asking us to "forgive" her or describe "the poor girl's fancy" and telling us how we must be "charitable" about her mistakes. The narrator's voice has become hers: "It was the house of darkness, the house of dumbness, the house of suffocation. Osmond's beautiful mind gave it neither light nor air. Osmond's beautiful mind, indeed, seemed to peep down from a small high window and mock her." Listen to those three "houses" and those two "beautiful minds." The rhetoric almost needs to be read aloud to hear its power. No longer do we look at her; now we are feeling with her. At last she realizes how intelligent Ralph is. "As intelligent as Gilbert? He was much more intelligent." I ask my students to "improve" any of the sentences. I tried one myself: "They were strangely married, at all events, and it was a horrible life." First, I discovered that in the New York edition James changed "awful" to "horrible," and that my "improvement"— taking out "at all events"—was no improvement at all.

Our old narrator is still there, a little, at least once, when Isabel realizes who her husband really is: "It was very simple, he despised her; she had no traditions and the moral horizon of a Unitarian minister." My students rarely get the joke in these dark days of defunct traditional faith and creeping latitudinarianism: "Poor Isabel, who had never been able to understand Unitarianism!" The line is so funny, so sad and sweet and consoling. Poor little rich girl.

What I am emphasizing, though, is that something remarkable has happened here: seated, Isabel stands on her own two feet. For the entire rest of the novel we are with her, and we see things her way. In chapter 42 it doesn't occur to me to pity or forgive her; I'm too busy admiring her. And in all subsequent chapters I watch her say and do things quite beyond me. In chapter 42 we see that our girl has indeed become a Lady, in the finest and richest sense of the word. No longer are we ahead of the game; we're right with her, every step of the way.

Critics have been awfully hard on Madame Merle. I should like to propose another way of looking at her. She explains to Isabel that "everyone bears some mark; even the hardest iron pots have a little bruise, a little hole somewhere. I've been shockingly chipped and cracked, I've been cleverly mended." "I'd give a great deal to be your age again. If I could only begin again—if I could have my life before me! The best part's gone, and gone for nothing. What have my talents brought me? Nothing but the need of using them still, to get through the hours, the years." Some readers find her so vile that they won't allow her even these moments of self-pity. But her description of herself is another Jamesian list of negatives, "What have I got? Neither husband, nor child, nor fortune, nor position, nor the traces of beauty I never had."

Very late in the game: "'Ah,' she said softly, 'if I had a child—!'" And when we finally discover that Pansy is her daughter, a much earlier line resonates with a sharp pang, Madame Merle's comment that "She doesn't like me." When we look back over every low and terrible thing Madame Merle has done—and she did do very low and very terrible things — we see she did them all for Pansy. At one point Isabel sees Madame Merle as a bust of Niobe, who, weeping, was turned into a stone column for her lost children—and still tears flow from the stone. I dislike her first name,

Serena, dislike even more her first first name, Geraldine, but I dislike them both because I always think of her real name as Madame Merle, a creature of supreme woe.

A bright, very opinionated, young woman in my seminar asked, "What's in it for Madame Merle to get Osmond to marry Isabel?—it makes no sense at all!" There are a few ways to answer that, but the one I chose was that Madame Merle saw in Isabel a way to protect Pansy from Osmond. Our most trustworthy social butterfly, the Countess Gemini, answers Isabel's question, "Why then did she want him to marry me?" by saying, "you had money; and because she believed you'd be good to Pansy." Amy puts the money first, but in point of fact (another list: Osmond has "no career, no name, no position, no fortune, no past, no future, no anything") Madame Merle thinks of Isabel as Pansy's stepmother *before* Isabel comes into her money.

Poor Henry James, Novelist. He had been pointing the whole book toward a showdown between the naive Isabel Archer and the duplicitous Madame Merle. And, when what he had most carefully and extensively prepared comes to its climax, he couldn't do it. He lamented, "I lose the 'great scene' between Madame Merle and Isabel." He had planned for Madame Merle ("in whose breast the suppressed feeling of maternity had long been rankling") "to break out with the cry that Pansy is her daughter." But he added, immediately and parenthetically, "(To be settled later whether this revelation is to be made by Mme. Merle herself, or by the Countess Gemini. Better on many grounds that it should be the latter)".

I always ask my class why he did that. The students say that Madame Merle could never say such a thing without losing her poise; she's not built that way, she is always the perfect social animal. James himself said as much: "I am not sure that it would not be best that the exposure of Mme. Merle should never be complete, and above all that she should not denounce herself. This would injure very much the impression I have wished to give of her profundity, her self-control, her regard for appearances." But there is something even more important. Were Madame Merle to disburden herself of her secret, what would her next step be? She would have to tell Osmond. But where's the fun in that? We would continue as we have done all along. Instead, in the scene as we have it, now for the first time Isabel knows something that they do not. And we are eager to see what she does with her newly found superior knowledge. We have seen what the guilty lovers have done to Isabel when she was in the dark. Of course, Isabel could take charge: "Oh, Gilbert, come here, my sweet, I want to discuss something with you." She does not do that, she does not do anything like it. Quite simply, she does something extraordinary: she does nothing at all. The focus is where it belongs, on Isabel's reaction, not on the news itself (or why Madame Merle stepped out of character). Matthiessen and Murdock assert, correctly, that James's "source of interest lay not in the events but in Isabel's sense of them." And the reader now eagerly awaits to see how a "Lady" will deal with this astonishing new problem.

She does what Maggie Verver will do, years later, in *The Golden Bowl*. With superior knowledge she never lets on, thereby sending the dark lady to the penal colony, America. Maggie says, "I know nothing on earth" and cites it as "the soldiers' watch-word at night." Near the end of *Portrait* James says, "Isabel would never accuse Madame Merle, never reproach her; perhaps because she never would give her the opportunity to defend herself." When Madame Merle tells Isabel that Ralph gave her the money and made her marriage to Osmond possible, Isabel quickly moves from the money to the marriage by saying, "I believed it was you I had to thank." Spoken like a true lady. And she is a "Lady" in a higher sense as well. When she visits her stepdaughter in the prison-convent, Pansy says, "Madame Merle has been here" and adds "I don't like Madame Merle!" Isabel hesitates, stops. Then she says, "You must never say that—that you don't like Madame Merle." Talk about grace under pressure!

The ending of *Portrait* presents many problems. James himself thought so, and wrote in his notebook that while "it may all be very true, very powerful, very touching," "the obvious criticism of course will be that it is not finished—that I have not seen the heroine to the end of her situation—that I have left her *en l'air*." And many readers are unhappy with the ending. In her fine essay, "Why Does Isabel Go Back to Osmond?" Dorothea Krook says,

I have heard it seriously argued that Isabel 'could after all have done something else'—walked out into freedom (like Nora in *A Doll's House,* presumably), or gone in for charitable works (like Dorothea Brooke in *Middlemarch*), or even perhaps taken a degree and become a pioneer in women's education, or whatever. The short answer to these bracing proposals is that Isabel Archer could have done none of these things.

So what should she have done? Is Ms. Krook's title posing the question correctly—does Isabel go back to *Osmond*? Horrible thought! By the end of the novel Osmond has revealed himself in his true colors; to return to him seems a particularly sadistic punishment for James to inflict on his heroine. Early in the book our narrator speaks of "the danger of keeping up the flag after the place has surrendered; a sort of behaviour so crooked as to be almost a dishonor to the flag." In the final pages, Caspar Goodwood says to Isabel, "It's too monstrous to think of you sinking back into misery." "It would be an insult to you to assume that you care for the look of the thing." By this point we want to cover our ears, the sound of Osmond's voice is impossible to bear: "What has become of Warburton? What does he mean by treating one like a trademan with a bill?" Or, worse:

I can't say much more for the great Warburton. When one really thinks of it, the cool insolence of that performance was something rare! He comes and looks at one's daughter as if she were a suite of apartments; he tries the door-handles and looks out of the windows, raps on the walls and almost thinks he'll take the place. Will you be so good as to draw up the lease? Then, on the whole, he decides that the rooms are too small; he doesn't think he could live on the third floor; he must look out for a *piano nobile.* And he goes away after having gotten a month's lodging in the poor little apartment for nothing.

This is a very creepy way to speak of one's daughter, as a piece of rental property, and a man "lodging in the poor little apartment for nothing"! Readers who resent James's political and social views should look carefully at this man, his most conservative, who snarls and spits at those whom he considers below him in class. When Isabel tells him that "she liked to know people who were as different as possible from herself," Osmond replies, "Why then don't you make the acquaintance of your washerwoman?" And of Henrietta he says, "I don't like at all to think she talks about me—I feel as I should feel if I knew the footman were wearing my hat." Osmond's exquisite sensibility has turned rancid; he is utterly hateful, beneath contempt. He tricked Isabel into marriage, lied to her, ruined her life—how on earth is Isabel bound to return to him, to *that*? Return to false accusations—we know Isabel has "done nothing of the sort" when Osmond accuses her of intercepting Lord Warburton's letter; and we know Pansy was the one who made it clear to Warburton that he should not ask her to marry him. James pulls out all the stops, which he surely would not have done if we were to think the marriage could be salvaged as anything other than perpetual punishment.

It also seems false to Isabel's most constant and cherished notion of her role in life: "She could never rid herself of the sense that unhappiness was a state of disease—of suffering as opposed to doing. To 'do'—it hardly mattered what—would therefore be an escape, perhaps in some degree a remedy." And on her voyage to the dying Ralph, Isabel thinks that "deep in her soul—deeper than any appetite for renunciation—was the sense that life would be her business for a long time to come." She thinks, "It couldn't be she was to live only to suffer. To live only to suffer"—note the exact repetition of the phrase—is anathema.

But, some apologists say, we must see two important factors in Isabel's returning to the clutches of the fiend. First, she is always reluctant to admit any error; as James says, "almost anything seemed preferable to repudiating the most serious act—the single sacred act—of her life." Divorce "would be an admission that their whole attempt had proved a failure." When Henrietta asks her, "Why don't you leave him?" Isabel says, "I can't publish my mistake. I don't think that's decent. I'd much rather die." Henrietta says, "You won't confess that you've made a mistake. You're too proud." But Isabel won't listen; "I don't know whether I'm too proud," but "one must accept one's deeds. I married him before all the world; I was perfectly free; it was impossible to do anything more deliberate." Admit to a mistake? "I can't announce it on the housetops." And we are in the social world of the 1870s. Even if Isabel could consider divorce, society would not let her do so. Millicent Bell says, "Practically speaking, divorce was still an alternative nearly unavailable to someone like Isabel when James wrote his novel. It was even legally difficult" in a time before "English law made provision for women as the injured party. Isabel had *no specific* outrage to charge Osmond with—he was neither an adulterer or a wife-beater."

My own sense of the rightness of the conclusion involves neither Osmond nor divorce. Henrietta says, "I don't see why you promised little Miss Osmond to go back." James repeatedly emphasizes that promise (and nothing is more sacred to Isabel than a promise). Leaving the convent, Isabel says to Pansy, "I won't desert you" and "yes, I'll come back." Her heart beating fast she goes so far as to propose, "Will you come away with me now?" So much for going back to Osmond. If Isabel can say that, she is capable of anything, even stealing his daughter away from him.

Second, Ralph puts it best—as Ralph always does—when on his dying day he says, "You're very young." Isabel says, "I feel very old," and he replies, "You'll grow young again. I don't believe that such a generous mistake as yours can hurt you for more than a little." It is important that Ralph—the smartest and best person in the book—trusts her. Now that she is a "Lady," it hardly matters what she does because we are assured she will do it well. Bell notes that "Caspar's kiss, the ritual gesture which ends so many novels, is present in all its power on the final page only to reveal its inability to provide an ending to the story of Isabel Archer." It wouldn't work, "it's just like a novel," as Isabel said at the very beginning. We see her, at Gardencourt, at the end; we saw her there at the beginning; in between, a lovely girl has become a profound lady, and we are ready to go with her wherever she must go.

Two critics have said the same thing: Richard Chase, "at the end of the book Isabel seems veritably to belong to the sisterhood of Hester Prynne" and Peter Buitenhuis, "the most obvious predecessor of Isabel in American fiction is Hester Prynne of *The Scarlet Letter.* At the end of the novel she, like Isabel, refuses the easy way out and chooses to return to the town where she had made her original decision and live out its consequences."

True enough, that deep family resemblance. Our national literature is notoriously male, celebrating the love of men and boys unchastened by "sivilization," a wild west show of masculine ego. We should remember, though, that two of the most resplendent and extraordinary figures in that literature are women. And we should remember, too, that like the men they are "citizens of somewhere else."

Chapter Eleven

Revision

The finest piece of criticism on Henry James I have ever read is F. O. Matthiessen's "The Painter's Sponge and Varnish Bottle," a study of James's revisions of the 1881 *Portrait of a Lady* for the New York edition of 1908. I should like to examine here a few alterations he does not touch upon.

The first thing to say about the five thousand revisions is that there are no plot changes. None. In that aspect of the book James was right the first time. Second, the prose style of the 1908 edition is decidedly not the prose style of *The Ambassadors*, *The Wings of the Dove*, and *The Golden Bowl* (all three of which were written before James revised the *Portrait*). I disagree entirely with an article by Paul Dean in which he says that "the eventual atrophy of James's art, the same tedium and lifelessness of his so-much-vaunted last phase" is also expressed in "his destructive tinkering with his early works, in which, having run out of material, he seems to have tried to exact revenge on his younger, more vital self by ruining what he had written." No, whatever one may think of James's work in his last "major phase," the revised *Portrait* has very little in common with the most remarkable feature of that period, its syntax. The grammar, the tempo, of *Portrait* retains its integrity.

I disagree, too, with Nina Baym's peculiar thesis that "the changes of 1908 overlaid and in places obliterated the coherence of the 1881 version"

161

and that "once recovered, the 1881 story may prove to be just as interesting as the version of 1908." I cannot understand the basis of such a claim or why Baym asserts that "in the revision, Madame Merle and Osmond lose such good qualities as they possess in the original, and are turned into wholly devious and shallow people. Their modicum of natural warmth and their substantial capacities disappear; both become mere swindlers." This is demonstrably false. Osmond's great speech to Isabel about her inheritance is changed from "Money is a great advantage," to "Money's a horrid thing to follow, but a charming thing to meet." He is lying in both statements, of course, but in the revision it is a much sounder lie, works so well on Isabel, and manages to include and to mean its exact opposite. Osmond has perfectly covered his tracks. Baym is surely wide of the mark when she complains that in 1908 Madame Merle "has no private side." In 1881 Madame Merle tells Osmond, "I believe you'll make me cry still," and in 1908 James gives her a wild new line, "I mean make me howl like a wolf." James also adds to "How do bad people end?" an italicized pun, "—especially as to their *common* crimes." And the last line of the scene, Mme. Merle's self-interrogatory, "Have I been so vile all for nothing?" is no longer "murmured to herself"; now, "she vaguely wailed." Mme. Merle has lost her "private side"? No, not at all; Mme. Merle's private side has been brought into a newer, sharper, more painful focus.

In 1908 almost all the characters are deepened and enlarged—Isabel and Ralph, of course, but also Caspar Goodwood, the Countess Gemini, and Pansy as well. When Isabel hears the sordid truth about Pansy's real mother, she says, in 1881, "Ah, poor creature"; in 1908 she says, "Ah, poor, poor woman." And in the 1881 "false to his wife" becomes in 1908 "false to his wife—and so very soon." Matthiessen has this one a little wrong, I think, when he comments that the addition "emphasizes Isabel's incurable innocence." On the contrary, it is the product of swift calculation and thoughtful maturity; Isabel gets it right and gets it right away.

When Mrs. Osmond meets Mme. Merle in the convent, for what will turn out to be their final interview, two brilliant revisions bring to the scene a heightened sense of drama, a compelling luridity: Mme. Merle's presence in the flesh "was suddenly, and rather awfully, like seeing a painted picture move." Even more shocking: "Her being there at all had the character of ugly evidence, of handwritings, of profaned relics, of grim things produced in court." These two images do not attenuate the story, they bring it to an almost hallucinatory new life.

Recently I set aside a week to read and think about all the five thousand changes and to consider their cumulative effect. Some of them are very funny: in the magazine serialization Henrietta and Mr. Bantling are "naive companions"; in 1881 they are "harmless confederates"; in 1908 they are "groping celibates." Ralph is, if anything, even funnier in 1908. When he misreads Henrietta ("I did think she was trying to attract me") in 1881 he says, "Excuse my superficiality," but in 1908 he says, "Forgive my depravity."

What struck me most, reading all the revisions together, was their certainty of tone. After Goodwood's first visit, we are told in 1881 that "Isabel was an excitable creature, and now she was much excited." In 1908 that is changed to "she was trembling—trembling all over. Vibration was easy to her, was in fact too constant with her, and she found herself now humming like a smitten harp." The new sentence is delightful in itself, but what interests me is the way it goes with another revision: in 1881, in the first paragraph of our famous chapter 42, Osmond's words "opened the door to agitation"; in 1908 they "suddenly made vibrations deep." My point is that "vibrations deep" and "smitten harp" *go together,* come from the same emotional place. As does a similar process: when Isabel is alone with Warburton at Gardencourt, she hears his words, and James adds in 1908 that they were "uttered with a breath of candour that was like the embrace of strong arms—that was like the fragrance straight in her face, and by his clean breathing lips, of she knew not what strange gardens, what charged airs." At the end of the book, James says that Isabel's response to Caspar's "mad" talk is to feel "the hot wind of the desert, at the approach of which the others dropped dead, like mere sweet airs of the garden." "Strange gardens" and "charged airs" early in the story—"airs of the garden" and "hot winds of the desert" late. When you read all the revisions together, you cannot escape the complexity of the changes and the way they work together seamlessly in a mutually enriching way.

Matthiessen is correct when he says that "it is notable that James's kinship here to Hawthorne becomes far more palpable in the final version." For example, Isabel wonders, after Ralph's death, if Mrs. Touchett "had not the desire for the recreation of grief" and needed to reach out "for some aftertaste of life, dregs of the banquet." Matthiessen claims that "the view of suffering, even the phrasing, recalls Hawthorne's *The Christmas Banquet.*" Undoubtedly so, for James clearly used that story just a few years earlier in *The Beast in the Jungle.* As I suggested in my first chapter, this is the Hawthorne to which the later James returns again and again for inspiration, especially when writing about death and the "dregs of the banquet, the testimony of pain."

Let me point briefly to a few instances where James changed a single word. They do in very small places what the larger changes do. In 1881, after Dan Touchett dies, Isabel puts out "her hand" to Ralph. In 1908 she puts out "her two hands." After Ralph dies, Isabel cries out to "Poor Aunt Lydia" in 1881; in 1908 she cries out to "Dear Aunt Lydia." The first one-word change gives us a more generous, spontaneous, and demonstrative Isabel; in the second she loves her aunt for herself as well as for her loss—"dear" is more intimate and knowing than "poor."

Some of these one-worders, of course, are just for fun; the "blue Pacific" of 1881 becomes the "green Pacific" in 1908 mainly, I think, so that we can enjoy Ralph's "I'm not sure the Pacific's so green as that." And the Countess Gemini's admonition to Isabel in 1881, "You have got such a pure mind" is more amusing and in character in 1908: "You've got such a beastly pure mind." The same goes for Amy's "she would stumble!" becoming "she'd dish herself!" and "wicked, for once" turned to "wicked, for the comfort of it, once."

James is always extremely careful when using actual names from the world of art, literature, and music. Here a "small Watteau" (1881) becomes a "small Lancret" (1908). The one I am most interested in involves Isabel's first scene with Madame Merle; at the piano Serena is "playing something of Beethoven—Isabel knew not what, but recognized Beethoven." And after a brief chat, Madame Merle sighs, smiles, and says, "I'm afraid there are moments in life when even Beethoven has nothing to say to us." In 1908 James changes "Beethoven" to "Schubert."

Why?

I suppose there are many possible answers (including the right one); I myself do not know enough to speak with any great authority, but I would begin by considering the nineteenth-century tendency to associate

Beethoven with a masculine revolutionary heroism and to associate Schubert with a certain kind of intimacy, femininity, and ambiguity. Beethoven is "big," colossally so, whereas, as Bernard Holland writes, "the real Schubert is about small rooms and friends." It is much more in Madame Merle's character for her to play Schubert instead of Beethoven. Madame Merle is the great deceiver, the consummate conniver, the mistress of "small rooms." She is not exactly a wit, but she is droll, and "Schubert" does make her line funnier—Beethoven *always* has something to say to us; to say Schubert doesn't is more knowing and world-weary. Isabel can't read the sophisticated little smile, and retreats to safety: "I should be so glad if you would play something more."

I find especially interesting both the biggest deletion James made and the biggest addition. The first, two pages in length, is a description of Gilbert Osmond just before he tells Isabel "I'm absolutely in love with you." James had said in 1881 that Osmond "had felt that any enterprise in which the chance of failure was at all considerable would never have an attraction for him; to fail would have been unspeakably odious, would have left an ineffaceable stain upon his life." This bully is a coward, and the game is over before it begins. We know suddenly what we should come to know gradually. "He had not gone about asking people whether they knew a nice little girl with a little money." Which, we can see, is not because it is wrong but because it violates the image of himself Osmond so desperately sustains. James is cutting out precisely what Baym claims he put in. In the same vein, "Madame Merle would have taken no pains to make Mr. Osmond acquainted with Mrs. Touchett's niece if Isabel had been as scantily dowered as when she first met her." Osmond "wanted only the best, and a portionless bride naturally would not have been the best." This is much too broad—it is in 1881, not 1908, that Madame Merle and Gilbert Osmond are "devious and shallow people," "mere swindlers."

When Madame Merle says, in 1881, that the English are "the finest people in the world," and in 1908 says they are "the most convenient in the world to live with," it is a step forward, rather than backward, entirely in character. Indeed, one might cry foul regarding the 1881 mention that "there was something very imperfect in Osmond's situation as it stood. He was a failure, of course; that was an old story; to Madame Merle's perception he would always be a failure." This is very close to misleading about their relationship. James saw, in 1908, that he should not have spoken of Madame Merle's "old-time interest in Osmond's affairs." The entire passage is cut.

The biggest addition, larger even than the final kiss, involves the Countess Gemini. It is quite amazing that James, twenty-five years after the fact, can so thoroughly create and enter into Amy Gemini's mind. He does not deface her portrait in the first edition, or violate in any way her flibberty-gibbet dialogue. All new in 1908 is her story of "the whole rigmarole" about Osmond's wife dying "of quite another matter and in quite another place" and her question, "Don't you see him looking at me, in silence, that way, to settle it?—that is to settle *me* if I should say anything." She's breezing along, the way she always does, but when she sees that Isabel has finally got it, "Pansy's wonderful aunt dropped—as, involuntarily, from the impression of her sister-in-law's face" and we see that the scatterbrain of 1881 is something of a "Lady" too, with a good heart and no deficit in the brains department when she watches Isabel sink to her seat. How can we not feel affection for this woman who declares, "My virtue has at any rate finally found itself exhausted"? In 1881 she said that Mme. Merle had "been wonderfully clever about Pansy"; in the revision "wonderfully clever" stays as it was, but she adds "she has been magnificent about Pansy." And the italicized "*intelligence*" gets completely rebuilt into " 'Besides, she has never had, about him,' the Countess went on, leaving Isabel to wince for it so tragically afterwards—'she *had* never had, what you might call any illusion of *intelligence*.' " And, with that, Amy's off and running again: Madame Merle " 'hates me, and her way of showing it is to pretend to be for ever defending me. When people say I've had fifteen lovers she looks horrified and declares that quite half of them were never proved.' "

This wonderful character profits immeasurably from her creator's new interest in her. One of the best moments in the book took twenty-five years to write—that is, took two ideas, twenty-five years apart, to complete.

A good student couldn't understand why I objected to his reading in Freudian terms Caspar Goodwood's exasperated cry to Isabel, "I can't penetrate you." My student said, "James does it all the time, and so do you—why can't *I*?" I said that *he* could, but Caspar couldn't—if Caspar "means" the pun, is Isabel supposed to say, "Yeah, right," or "don't go there," or what? In

1876 a man can't "penetrate" a woman out loud and to her face. The student and I went on to discuss Caspar's claim in the final scene that "it's too monstrous" to think of Isabel going back to Osmond, "of going to open your mouth to that poisoned air." He implores her: "You've got no children." But she does have a daughter, a stepdaughter, who is in grave danger of being manipulated into a life of unhappiness. Isabel is prepared to do anything for her. Goodwood doesn't understand that, so intent is he on getting Isabel to realize "you must save what you can of your life; you mustn't lose it all simply because you've lost a part." She must choose him over "the bottomless idiocy of the world." Upon which he gives her the deepest kiss in American literature.

Millicent Bell suggests that "plot itself, it may be said, is describable in sexual terms. The arousal of tension, the achievement of climax, the attainment of pleasure, and the dissolution of desire itself in the subsidence to quiescence—these phrases describe the trajectory of a story." Bell moves directly to Caspar's kiss and Isabel's running from it. "Kiss" seems too small a word for what "wrapped her about, lifted her off her feet, while the very taste of it, as of something potent, acrid and strange, forced open her set teeth": it

> was like white lightning, a flash that spread, and spread again, and stayed; and it was extraordinarily as if, while she took it, she felt each thing in his hard manhood that had least pleased her, each aggressive fact of his face, his figure, his presence justified of its intense identity and made one with this act of possession. So had she heard of those wrecked under water following a train of images before they sink.

It is to read the text literally, not in Freudian terms, to say that this is an orgasm, and that it is a woman's orgasm ("a flash that spread, and spread again, and stayed"). It is no idle exercise in symbolism to read that Caspar's "hard manhood" is "justified of its intense identity and made one with this act of possession." And, judging from Isabel's response to this little Death, we can surely forget all about the dumb charge that she is "frigid." Nothing like this has ever happened to her before, and we feel that if she goes back to Osmond it never will again. James invented it all—for the first time—when he was sixty-four—the most passionate, powerful, and daring unto reckless of all the five thousand changes.

Hawthorne in 1862. Photograph by the Mathew Brady Studio.
Courtesy, National Archives and Records Administration.

James, Culver Pictures.

Chapter Twelve

"The Wings of Experience"

I conclude with the profoundly American quality of our two citizens of somewhere else. Consider these testimonials:

Ralph Waldo Emerson, approaching his twenty-first birthday, in his journal: "I make it my best boast that I am a citizen of a far country."

V.S. Pritchett, *A Cab at the Door:* "I became a foreigner. For myself that is what a writer is—a man living on the other side of a frontier."

Henry James, Sr., to Emerson in the fall of 1860, after a dinner of Boston's Saturday Club at the Parker House: Hawthorne "had the look all the time, to one who didn't know him, of a rogue who suddenly finds himself in a company of detectives."

Tocqueville, *Democracy in America* (1835):
America has hitherto produced very few writers of distinction; it possesses no great historians and not a single eminent poet. The inhabitants of that country look upon literature properly so called with a kind of disapprobation; and there are towns of second-rate importance in Europe in which more literary works are annually published than in the twenty-four states of the Union put together.

Ford Madox Ford, *Thus to Revisit* (1921):

In, I think, the year before the war, I published a monograph on the works of Henry James, and this work was received by the Press with a violence of disapproval that can seldom be equalled. I have frequently asked myself why this was? I can only imagine that I was suddenly hated because I hatefully pointed out that this great man was an American. And yet, at this moment, I insist on his Americanism.

Henry James in an 1867 letter to Thomas Sergeant Perry: "I think that to be an American is an excellent preparation for culture."

Nathaniel Hawthorne in "The Custom-House": "I am in the realm of quiet ... I am a citizen of somewhere else."

Willy on Harry: "He is a native of the James family, and has no other country."

Harry to Willy (1888): "I aspire to write in such a way that it would be impossible to an outsider to say whether I am at any given moment an American writing about England or an Englishman writing about America (dealing as I do with both countries), and so far from being ashamed of such an ambiguity I should be exceedingly proud of it, for it would be highly civilized."

Over the years I have wondered what Nathaniel Hawthorne must have thought and felt when he read the early reviews of *The Scarlet Letter* in which critics complained that Pearl wasn't a "real" child. I hear that objection even today, in some of my student papers. Usually mentioned is this passage in chapter VI:

Her mother, while Pearl was yet an infant, grew acquainted with a certain peculiar look, that warned her when it would be labor thrown away to insist, persuade, or plead. It was a look so intelligent, yet inexplicable, so perverse, sometimes so malicious, but generally accompanied by a wild flow of spirits, that Hester could not help questioning, at such moments, whether Pearl was a human child. She seemed rather an airy sprite, which, after playing its fantastic sports for a little while upon the cottage floor, would flit away with a mocking smile.

Hester feels the impulse "to snatch her to her bosom, with a close pressure and earnest kisses,—not so much from overflowing love, as to assure herself that Pearl was flesh and blood, and not utterly delusive." The reason I wonder about Hawthorne's response is that this "unreal" child was his own. In his notebook for July 30, 1849, he wrote of Una:

> there is something that almost frightens me about the child—I know not whether elfish or angelic, but, at all events, supernatural. She steps so boldly into the midst of everything, shrinks from nothing, has such a comprehension of everything, seems at times to have but little delicacy, and anon shows that she possesses the finest essence of it; now so hard, now so tender; now so perfectly unreasonable, soon again so wise. In short, I now and then catch an aspect of her, in which I cannot believe her to be my own human child, but a spirit strangely mingled with good and evil, haunting the house where I dwell.

Those 1850 reviewers' doubts about the human reality of the "airy sprite" surely arise from the way Pearl violates the Victorian stereotype of children as both miniature adults and vessels of angelic purity.

In our post-Freudian world have we gained anything? In *Dearest Beloved* (1993), T. Walter Herbert asserts that Hawthorne "found his daughter's thighs and buttocks sexually appealing, and as she romped about the house she revealed what he wanted—yet did not want—to see." Herbert asks, "Does she thrust up her anus as a gesture of defiance?" Gulp. Again, "when Una Hawthorne was five years old she was given repeated indications of her father's revulsion at her taking pleasure in her own body, especially when this aroused him sexually." Herbert concludes that this "invasion of a young girl's sexuality by her father's disgust becomes tantamount to rape."

Where to begin with such a critical catastrophe? I can find no evidence—external or internal—that Hawthorne's feelings for his five-year-old daughter are anything at all like Mr. Herbert's feverish "analysis" of them. Una is a model for Pearl, clearly so, and Hester's feeling for her daugh-

ter comes straight from Hawthorne's feeling for his. But the sexual psychob-
abble is all Herbert's. Following Hawthorne all the way to Rome, Herbert
teases us with suggestive questions: "Did Louisa take off all her clothes for
Nathaniel? Did he take off his clothes for her? Did they have sex?"

I should like to examine some similarly absurd propositions about the origins of Gilbert Osmond in *The Portrait of a Lady.* The ideas lack the lurid
sexuality of Herbert's reading of little Una Hawthorne and her pe-
dophile lech of a father, but they are preposterous all the same. I would
agree with Oscar Cargill that "Osmond is Henry James's most completely
evil character." Yvor Winters hated Osmond so much that he misspelled
his name, "Osmund," all through his essay, and declared that the aesthete
was so unrelievedly Gothic that he threw the whole novel off-balance.
Leon Edel says that Osmond, "like Catherine Sloper's father in *Washington
Square,* expresses one side of Henry James himself": "Osmond's selfishness and his 'demonic imagination' belong in all probability to James's
'buried life,' some part of which he concealed even from himself, but
which emerged in the writing of this character." "In all probability"? To
be sure, all characters have to come from *some*where in the writer's imagination, and, yes, not infrequently "concealed even from himself." But it is
surely a big jump to say, as Edel does, that "James put into Osmond his
own high ambition and drive to power." Frankly, this Osmond sounds to
me more like Leon Edel than Henry James. And once people get started
down that road it is difficult to call them back. Fred Kaplan, for example,
insists that "Osmond is a distorted but revealing depiction of Henry's feelings of repressed erotic attraction to William" and constitutes "Henry's revenge on William for his brother's lifelong boasts of manly superiority." I
think Kaplan takes far too seriously Willy's boast to his kid brother: "*I* play
with boys who curse and swear!" Henry said that William "had gained
such an advance of me in his sixteen months' experience of the world before mine began that I never for all the time of childhood and youth in
the least caught up with him and overtook him. He was always around the
corner and out of sight." The complicated relationship between the two
brothers is beautifully analyzed in Matthiessen's "group biography," *The
James Family.* Gilbert Osmond is William James? Surely not. Perhaps Kaplan senses his claim is not altogether convincing, even if "Osmond, like

William, has close-cropped hair, a short-clipped sharp beard, a thin angular body, and bright, intelligent eyes." Kaplan says, "as much as Osmond embodies Henry's revenge on William," (!) he is also Pansy, a child "shaped by a cleverly expressive, totally controlling father," and that the fathers in James's work "are unreliable, deadly, or both." Like Dan Touchett? Kaplan concludes that "the world of *Portrait* is a threatening, often deadly world of repression and annihilation; it is a nightmare novel" and "Isabel Archer and Pansy Osmond are Jamesian self-portraits."

These are grotesque, screwball linkages between art and personal life. Sometimes, though, in the right hands, the linkages can be brilliantly apt and instructive. Take James himself—in the essay on Hawthorne for Warner's 1896 volume, he is clearly reminding us of Hester Prynne when he says that "what Hawthorne encountered he instinctively embroidered, working it over with a fine, slow needle." And I agree with Philip Rahv's estimate of the autobiographical in *The Portrait of a Lady:* "If James's relation to his native land is in question, then more is to be learned from this young woman's career than from any number of discursive statements quoted from his letters, essays, and autobiographies." Fair enough. And so, too, is Richard Poirier's claim that "Isabel's career can be viewed as an enactment of the various concerns which James feels in the process of creating her. Isabel's ambition is James's achievement. One recognizes that James's vocabulary when talking about fiction is identical to that used to describe Isabel's ambition and hopes." Such a statement strikes me as both true and helpful (helpful because it is true). Millicent Bell comments on autobiographical elements in *Portrait:* the house in Albany is very much like the James house there, "including the adjoining primary school and the taste 'of accessible garden peaches' associated with his own grandmother's house in Albany." Henry's memory of that Dutch house becomes Isabel's house.

For my own part in this attempt to describe accurately how autobiographical events and real people become fictional, I note that Isabel's father, like James's, "had squandered a substantial good fortune," and that both Isabel and Henry "had been sent to superficial schools, kept by the French, from which at the end of a month, they had been removed in tears," and that "before Isabel was fourteen, her father had transported them three times across the Atlantic."

Isabel's "great desire for knowledge" is very much like Henry's "gaping":

> She had an immense curiosity about life and was constantly staring and wondering. She carried within herself a great fund of life, and her deepest enjoyment was to feel the continuity between the movement of her own soul and the agitation of the world. For this reason she was fond of seeing great crowds and large stretches of country, of reading about revolutions and wars, of looking at historical pictures.

Here, Isabel *is* Henry. And in her "deepest enjoyment" she fails to find the appeal of Caspar Goodwood; he lacks "easy consonance with the deeper rhythms of life." That's what Isabel is still looking for at the end of the book when she sees a London crowd as "a mighty spectacle in which there was something that touched her." Yes, Henry James put a great deal of himself into Isabel. And we don't need to play any games to see it.

Zenobia says to the poet, Miles Coverdale, "This long while past you have been following up your game, groping for human emotion in the dark corners of the heart." She attacks him because he is a writer: "Ah, I perceive what you are about! You are turning this whole affair into a ballad." To do that, to turn life into art, constitutes for both Hawthorne and James a sort of criminal curiosity. I think of Philip Roth's terrible quip: "Nothing bad can happen to a writer; it's all material." In this regard, a major meaning of my title "Citizens of Somewhere Else," is that these two American writers defined themselves as living to some extent in the land of writing itself, the foster home of the imagination. Nathaniel Hawthorne frequently concocted writer fables: "The Artist of the Beautiful," "Drowne's Wooden Image," "The Devil in Manuscript." And so did James—"The Real Thing," a perfect little investigation into the requirements of art and the demands of life, and several stories specifically about writers: "The Lesson of the Master," "Greville Fane," "The Figure in the Carpet," "The Middle Years," "The Death of the Lion."

In Hawthorne's preface to *Mosses from an Old Manse* he ransacks his "predecessor's library" for "any living thought, which should burn like a coal of fire, or glow like an inextinguishable gem." He poked around for stuff that might provide an opportunity for imaginative flight, as in the

"Custom-House" scene when he finds, with the help of Mr. Surveyor Pue, the scarlet letter itself. And in his preface to *The Snow Image* he identifies himself in stark terms as "a person who has been burrowing, to his utmost ability, into the depths of our common nature, for the purpose of psychological romance." He is Paul Pry, and he turns the Old Manse itself into his own definition of romance: "The glimmering shadows, that lay half-asleep between the doors of the house and the public highway, were a kind of spiritual medium, seen through which, the edifice had not quite the aspect of belonging to the material world." The odd thing here is that writing—narrative art—involves spiritual delinquency of a profound kind. It can also produce superficial results. Hawthorne confesses in "The Custom-House" that "I took shame to myself for having been so long a writer of idle stories." A splendid passage of American autobiography is Hawthorne's dismayed imagination of what the ghosts of his stern ancestors say of him: "A writer of storybooks! What kind of business in life—what mode of glorifying God, or being serviceable to mankind in his day and generation,—may that be? Why, the degenerate fellow might as well have been a fiddler!"

Miles Coverdale is, as James puts it in *Hawthorne,* "a portrait of a man, in a word, whose passions are slender, whose imagination is active, and whose happiness lies, not in doing, but in perceiving—half a poet, half a critic, and all a spectator." James concludes that some of Hawthorne's companions "took, I believe, rather a gruesome view of his want of articulate enthusiasm, and accused him of coming to the place as a sort of intellectual vampire, for purely psychological purposes." "He sat in a corner, they declared, and watched the inmates when they were off their guard, analysing their characters, and dissecting the amiable ardour, the magnanimous illusions, which he was too cold-blooded to share." There's the magic word, "cold-blooded." It is a condition about which both Hawthorne and James had very deep, contradictory feelings. Withdrawing from the human community, separating oneself from others, is what a writer does and who he is—a vague, slippery fellow at best. And at his worst,

He had lost his hold of the magnetic chain of humanity. He was no longer a brother-man, opening the chambers or the dungeons of our common nature by the key of holy sympathy, which gave him a right to share in all its secrets; he was now a cold observer, looking on mankind as the subject of his experiment, and, at length, converting man and woman to be his puppets, and pulling the wires that moved them to such degrees of crime as were demanded for his study.

Thus Ethan Brand became a fiend.

A writer.

But these evil fellows tell us truths we had not known before. Miles Coverdale is a most reliable narrator: his account of returning to town, living in a hotel, looking out the back window of his room—all that refractory emotion—is beautifully rendered. In "The Hotel," "The Boarding-House," and "Zenobia's Drawing-Room," Coverdale becomes a Transparent Eyeball and Transcendental Ear, roaming, spying, peeking, listening. No wonder he ends up as a "frosty bachelor."

I have mentioned Max Beerbohm's verbal caricature of James, "The Mote in the Middle Distance." Equally delightful is a visual one, the cartoon in which James is pictured as an elderly, portly voyeur, kneeling down to listen at the keyhole of a hotel room beside which stand a pair of man's boots and a pair of woman's boots, waiting to be shined. There's a writer for you. Millicent Bell has described "a whole family of Jamesian stories illustrating moral and emotional defection in the aesthetic personality," and he was "always fascinated by the paradoxical combination, in particular, of refinement and intelligence with moral callousness."

In this regard I have often wondered about the weird, heartbreaking note found among Constance Fenimore Woolson's papers after her suicide in 1894: "To imagine a man spending his life looking for and waiting for his 'splendid moment?' 'Is this my moment?' 'Will this state of things bring it to me?' But the moment never comes." Nobody, so far as I know, has explained exactly what this is and precisely how it is related to *The Beast in the Jungle*. The half-dozen assessments I have read are too sketchy for me. I want to know why this is in *her* notebook, a perfect description of *his* story, almost a decade before he wrote it. What did James really mean when he wrote to Margaret Brooks that Constance had been "a close and valued friend of mine—a friend of many years with whom I was extremely intimate and to whom I was greatly attached." Edel notes the oddly *un*-Jamesian phrase "with whom I was extremely intimate." And we cannot avoid hearing her notebook entry in his, seven years later, "A man haunted by the fear, more and more throughout life, that *something will happen to him*; he doesn't quite know what." Did James for a time "live with" Woolson, during their daily expeditions in Florence in 1880-81? Was Woolson herself, as some critics have suggested, the model for May Bartram? When James learned of Woolson's death, he traveled from De Vere Gardens in London to Venice to help with the sorting and packing of her things (Mrs. Benedict, Constance's sister, wrote in her diary that "we could not have gone through it without him"). Or was James, as Edel suggests, merely eager to recover his letters to her? As I write this, I'm beginning to feel like the narrator of *The Aspern Papers,* but I suspect that Woolson's note could provide one of the most painful and revealing instances of the problem I am exploring here, the relationship between the lived life and the achieved art.

To tell the truth, though, I don't really want to know. One of my favorite words in *Huckleberry Finn* is "fantods." I sort of knew what it meant, but in one heavily annotated edition the word was footnoted, and before I sensed what I was doing and stopped my eyes, they had slid to the bottom of the page, "Delirium Tremens." But I don't *want* the D.T.s—I'm a "fantods" man. Why should I substitute a dull little answer for a nice little question? My idea of a great work was well put by that noble literary critic, Albert Einstein, "The most beautiful thing we can experience is the mysterious." I think the best critics do their work in the spirit of what Keats found in Shakespeare's mind, "*Negative Capability,* that is, when a man is capable of being in uncertainties, mysteries, doubts, without an irritable reaching after fact and reason."

Indeed, how far can we go in trying to find answers to our questions—without becoming "writers" ourselves? We are presented here with a distinctly American idea of authorship, unlike anything in French, Italian, or English literature, in which centuries of great works precede us. American literature *begins* in Hawthorne's time, and Hawthorne's example was central to James's sense of his vocation. But I fear a great error potentially lurking here. In another place I have dissented from Michael T. Gilmore's proposal that Hester Prynne and Arthur Dimmesdale are two different types of American writers: Hester is "the first full-length representation in American literature of the alienated modern artist," and Dimmesdale "is a type of the artist for whom fame and popularity are everything." No, I think the two lovers have quite enough trouble on their hands in the seventeenth century without being turned into nine-teenth-century "writers." I have also objected, and at some length, to the various critical readings of Melville's Bartleby as a "writer." Sure, Bartleby is a "scrivener," but in the lawyer's office he is a nineteenth-century Xe-rox machine. He's not a "writer."

My problem in working this out was that two of my favorite Melville critics, Newton Arvin and Richard Chase, took virtually for granted that Melville saw his own imperiled authorship in Bartleby. The same is true here: two of my favorite James critics eagerly see *The Beast in the Jungle* in just the terms I am reluctant to apply: Fred Dupee ("Marcher's losses are an exaggeration of the losses suffered by James in his dedication to the life of sensibility and art, his ultimate art fable") and Irving Howe (" 'The Beast in the Jungle' can be read as an instance of a writer bril-liantly savaging his own premises"). Well, then, couldn't one say that Strether is a "writer," and that *The Ambassadors* is a story about a provin-cial novelist who, at middle age, comes into full command of his cos-mopolitan "subject"? Or take that loopy Governess in *The Turn of the Screw*; she's a crackerjack "writer" of suspense novels, she does everything an accomplished practitioner of that genre should do with character and plot (and she has quite a distinctive prose style, too). I guess my reluctance to see "writer" is somehow connected to my uneasiness about seeing characters as really "Gay"—it's not an approach, it is an agenda, and we follow that agenda as much as we follow the story. Our interest in the work is by definition narrowed rather than enlarged.

These criticisms remind me of the land-locked criticism of the 1950s in which every writer in the New England Renaissance was writing about writing. When figures like Emerson and Thoreau are turned into Symbolists, they lose their profound conviction and their social reference. I think John Marcher suffers from a general failure of being, not writer's block. We no longer require our critics to be accurate; we ask them to be "interesting." And before you know it, Hawthorne is sexually involved with his five-year-old daughter, John Marcher is gay, Pansy Osmond is Henry James, and Gilbert Osmond is William James.

But Dupee and Howe do have a legitimate point. John Marcher is not himself a *writer*, a direct extension of James's dilemma as one caught between life and art, but his story is the master "figure in the carpet" of James's work in this mode. We should think not of single characters but of the work itself, the structure of the imagination. One might say that given the tensions at work in James's oeuvre, one can see how James, of all people, would create a John Marcher—not a failed writer in fictional disguise but the character written by an author who chose the story of a failed being as an extension of his own dilemma. Marcher is something *like* a writer, examining himself voyeuristically at a distance, or examining what could have been himself had he not been immersed in the unwritten story of his life. In other words, there is a degree to which people are "writers" when they become cold-blooded and analytical of themselves and their relationships. They have, one might say, continuous out-of-body experiences; they do not live, they "dream of living," which is what writers do.

At the beginning of this chapter I quoted a sentence from Henry James, Sr.'s letter to Emerson about a dinner of Boston's Saturday Club at the Parker House; it seems appropriate here to quote more of it, the absolutely wonderful description of Hawthorne:

> It was so pathetic to see him, contented, sprawling Concord owl that he was and always has been, brought blindfolded into that brilliant daylight, and expected to wink and be lively like any little dapper Tommy Titmouse or Jenny Wren. How he buried his eyes in his plate, and ate with such a voracity that no person should dare ask him a question!
>
> My heart broke for him as that attenuated Charles Norton kept putting forth his long antennae towards him, stroking his face, and trying whether his eyes were shut. It was heavenly to see him persist in ignoring Charles Norton, and shutting his eyes against his spectral smiles: eating his dinner and doing absolutely nothing but that, and then going home to his Concord den to fall upon his knees, and ask his heavenly Father why it was that an owl couldn't remain an owl, and not be forced into the dimension of a canary. I have no doubt that all the tenderest angels saw to his care that night, and poured oil into his wounds more soothing than gentlemen ever know.

I don't know if Lionel Trilling would call this "our" Hawthorne, but it surely is mine. And I do not scoff, as some readers do, at the question Hawthorne's close friend George Hilliard put to him: "How come it is that with so thoroughly healthy an organization as you have, you have such a taste for the morbid anatomy of the human heart, and such knowledge of it too." It is an honest, interesting question. Towards the end, Hawthorne wrote that his had been "a life of much smoulder and scanty fire." How could such an intensely, morbidly private man be what Charles Wilkins Webber in the *American Whig Review* called him—"national in subject, in treatment, and in manner"—even if he had been born, as he was, on the Fourth of July? For quite a long time he wanted to publish "Seven Tales of *My Native Land*." He is a most curious figure: Lizzie Peabody gushed "he is handsomer than Lord Byron" and according to family legend a gypsy woman saw him walking in the woods near Bowdoin, and asked, "Are you a man or an angel?"

Back in the late sixties and early seventies, when I'd get all worked up about this in the classroom, some student would usually bring me right back down to earth, by asking me, 'Do you agree with his politics?' Those flower children had read "The Maypole of Merrymount," and they knew whose "side" Hawthorne was on. I'd tell the dull truth—that both Nathaniel Hawthorne and Henry James stand, politically, way to the right of me. But what does that mean? I find no contradictions between leftist political convictions and conservative esthetics. I don't really care about what Hawthorne said in his campaign biography of Franklin Pierce; his political convictions are not at all what I read him for. To me the essential Hawthorne, the valuable Hawthorne, is his anguished cry to Longfellow, "For the last ten years I have not lived, but only dreamed of living." What interests me is his painful complaint to Horatio Bridge, "I detest this town so much that I hate to go into the streets or to have people see me." What a thing to say! And it is a shock to read his growl, during those "lonely chamber" years, "We do not even *live* at our house!" If Hawthorne's is a "national voice," it is the voice of introversion, claustrophobia, unbearable loneliness. He felt that he lived in a prison, and there are funny little touches associated with his incarceration: he wrote of his room in his mother's house, "In this dismal and squalid chamber—*Fame* was won." Sophia made him delete "and squalid." There is something exasperatingly amusing when he cries to his publisher, "I wish God had given me the faculty of writing a sunshiny book." That's not ironic; he really did wish that. He never got used to his solitary estate, or settled for it, and his inbred melancholy kept surprising him. Leslie Fiedler suggests that Hawthorne

> must be read finally neither as one figure not the other, but as a *double* man: not merely the kind of person who writes with one part of himself and lives with another, but double to the heart of his work and his existence. He seems always to be looking over his own shoulder. At his worst, he falls into mere playfulness or sentimental evasion; but at his best, he approaches the profound double view which lies at the heart of tragedy.

Have I insisted too much on Hawthorne's being "a citizen of somewhere *else*"? James said in 1879 "Hawthorne was at home in the early New England history; he had thumbed its records and he had breathed its air, in whatever odd receptacles this somewhat pungent compound still lurked. He was fond of it, and he was proud of it, as any New Englander must be, measuring the part of that handful of half-starved fanatics who formed his earliest precursors, in laying the foundation of a mighty empire."

The closer you get to Hawthorne the farther he moves away. In his desperate last years the same number keeps coming up: in "The Custom-House" he wrote that he took walks "seldom and reluctantly"; in the late fragment of *The Dolliver Romance* his hero could be seen "walking the streets seldom and reluctantly."

He talks constantly about the broken "magnetic chain of humanity" and how he has "broken his connecting links with the net-work of human life." The most terrifying face he sees in a mirror is always his beautiful own. Seeking innocence, he invariably finds its opposite. The world is thoroughly undependable, and the earth opens up to swallow him. It happens without warning: a little rural ramble becomes a tragic journey. He says in his notebook in 1842,

> I took a walk through the woods, yesterday afternoon, to Mr. Emerson's, with a book which Margaret Fuller had left behind her, after a call on

Saturday eve. I missed the nearest way, and wandered into a very se-
cluded portion of the forest—for forest it might justly be called, so
dense and sombre was the shade of the oaks and pines. Once I wandered into a tract so overgrown with bushes and underbrush that I could
scarcely force a passage through. Nothing is more annoying than a walk
of this kind—to be tormented to death by an innumerable host of petty
impediments; it incenses and depresses me at the same time. Always
when I flounder into the midst of a tract of bushes, which cross and in-
tertwine themselves about my legs, and brush my face, and seize hold of
my clothes with a multitudinous gripe—always, in such a difficulty, I
feel as if it were almost as well to lie down and die in rage and despair, as
to go one step further.

I hope I am not doing what I warned against earlier in this chapter when
I say that this marvelous passage is about Hawthorne the "writer" caught
in a world he is trying to make meaning of. Its "details" thwart his mind.
Everything's "real" and everything's symbolic at the same time. It is what
David Van Leer, Richard Brodhead, and I emphasize about the imaginative texture of *The Scarlet Letter,* at once physical and spiritual. When
"petty impediments" become a "multitudinous gripe," we have an example of what makes Nathaniel Hawthorne permanently intriguing.

Emerson wrote in his journal for 1864,

Yesterday, May 23, we buried Hawthorne in Sleepy Hollow, in a pomp
of sunshine and verdure, and gentle winds. A large company filled the
church and the grounds of the cemetery. All was so bright and quiet that
pain or mourning was hardly suggested, and Holmes said to me that it
looked like a happy meeting. I thought there was a tragic element in the
event, that might be more fully rendered,—in the painful solitude of the
man, which, I suppose, could not longer be endured, and he died of it.

Early on, Henry James said, "That New England should be my fate was
a danger after all escaped." Late in life, on a ten-month return trip to
America, he discovered America "to be a spacious vacancy," and wrote to
his sister-in-law Alice, after William's death, "I could come back to

America (could be carried back on a stretcher) to die—but never, never to live." America is provincial and backward. Yet he also sees in it an idea of a sublime country—in Richard Hofstadter's epigram, "a country conceived in perfection and dedicated to progress."

Henry James knows a lot about a lot, especially when dealing with his two great subjects, money and sex, and he knows so much about class and family and psychology; he is a wonderful travel writer, a real giant in criticism (not just literary criticism, he is a very fine critic of painting), an excellent historian, a master of epistolary art (thousands of the most beautiful letters ever written, to men and to women and to young people of all sexes, letters which simply take your breath away), a great editor of his own work (those five thousand changes in *The Portrait of a Lady*, 99 percent of which profoundly enrich the novel). It simply wears you out thinking about how well he did all the things he did. He seems to have taken his own advice: "Try to be one of the people on whom nothing is lost."

But if we go back to that famous list in *Hawthorne* we can find a splendid joke on Henry James. Stephen Donadio quotes Percy Lubbock's introduction to James's *Letters*:

> with much that is common ground among educated people of our time and place he was never really in touch. One has only to think of the part played, in the England he frequented, by school and colleges, by country-homes, by church and politics and professions, to understand how much of the ordinary consciousness was closed to him.

Donadio remarks, "The list of aspects of that life which, Lubbock claims, were 'closed' to James significantly echoes the novelist's own legendary inventory of all that was lacking in the United States of Hawthorne's time . . . those complex institutional configurations and dense tissues of social circumstance."

That is true, and I see no reason to quarrel with the generally accepted notion that late in his life James "blossomed," in the sense that great masses of repressed feeling gradually came into remarkable bloom. I would add only that its most striking manifestation is frequently keyed to "the complex fate of being an American." For example, James's most notorious book review, as Matthiessen says, "is that of *Drum Taps*. It is as wrong-headed in its judgments as a destructive piece by a self-confident reviewer of twenty-two could well be." Late in life, James reversed himself. Edith Wharton describes an extraordinary evening when James visited her at "The Mount" in 1905: when someone spoke of Whitman

> it was a joy to me to discover that James thought him, as I did, the greatest American poet. *Leaves of Grass* was put into his hands, and all that evening we sat rapt while he wandered from 'The Song of Myself' to 'When lilacs last in the dooryard bloomed' (when he read 'Lovely and soothing Death,' his voice filled the hushed room like an organ adagio), and thence let himself be lured on to the mysterious music of 'Out of the Cradle,' reading, or rather crooning it in a mood of subdued ecstasy. I had never before heard poetry read as he read it; and I never have since.

For those who find this rather over-full and sentimental, Miss Wharton adds a delightful little touch:

> We talked long that night of *Leaves of Grass,* tossing back and forth to each other treasure after treasure; but finally James, in one of his sudden humorous drops from the heights, flung up his hands and cried out with the old stammer and twinkle: 'Oh, yes, a great genius; undoubtedly a very great genius! Only one cannot help deploring his too-extensive acquaintance with the foreign languages.'

In *Notes of a Son and Brother* (1914) James looked back half a century to 1864, when he was six weeks shy of his twenty-first birthday, and recalled his anguished "loyal cry" at hearing of Hawthorne's death. We see in them both a heroic effort to locate some America, some imaginative New-Found-Land whose spokesman they so wanted to be. Yvor Winters warned how easy it is "to exaggerate the importance of nationalism in literature," but the specifically American quality of James's genius is crucially important to a full understanding of his achievement and his place in our culture.

F. W. Dupee says that "what surprises us about James—and would surprise us more if we did not know that the same was true of Hawthorne—is the extent to which his career was rooted in the conviction of inexperience." "The conviction of inexperience" is an apt characterization of the little brother who expressed his chagrin that "all boys I found were rather difficult to play with." He complained, "They were so *other*—that was what I felt." A small boy and o*thers.* Throughout James's life one sees a very strong, almost crippling, sense of estrangement. James reminds us of Hawthorne when he writes to Morton Fullerton in October 1900 about "the essential loneliness" of his life, and he goes on to say it is "the deepest thing" about him.

Both Hawthorne and James had an extraordinary capacity for grief, and they mourned their loved ones in enormously touching ways. Hawthorne wrote, at his mother's death,

> I did not expect to be so much moved at the time, but I was moved to kneel down close to my mother, and take her hand, and then I found the tears slowly gathering in my eyes. I tried to keep them down, but it would not be—I kept filling up, till, for a few moments, I shook with sobs. For a long time I knelt there, holding her hand; and surely it is the darkest hour I have ever lived.

Compare that with Harry's words after Willy's death: "I sit heavily stricken and in darkness—for from far back in dimmest childhood he had been my ideal Elder Brother, and I still, through all the years, saw in him, even as a small timorous boy yet, my backer, my authority, and my pride." What finer tribute can a younger brother provide? Both writers eloquently convey a bottomless sorrow.

My title for this final chapter, "The Wings of Experience," is from *The Beast in the Jungle,* where John Marcher finally realizes why his whole spiritually and sexually expatriate life had been so inward, so earthbound: "It hadn't come to him, the knowledge, on the wings of experience." One could use that sentence to describe James's experience—*in*experience—of his "Native Land" and his more or less permanent exile from it. He realized his own situation in Ralph Touchett's witty remark, "Ah, one doesn't give up one's country any more than one gives up one's grandmother. It's antecedent to choice." James confessed to Hamlin Garland, "If I were to live my life over again, I would be an American. I would steep myself in America, I would know no other land. I would study its beautiful side. I have lost touch with my own people and I live here alone." Which was not true, of course, as he knew. He had done the right thing. Even more than Hawthorne, who said it, James was "a citizen of somewhere else." But Henry James, like his powerful predecessor, was fatally, utterly, inescapably American. And he would have been genuinely pleased, he would have taken it as an honor, to be so identified.

A Note on Sources

For the convenience of the reader, not to mention my own, I have used Norton Critical Editions wherever possible. For three reasons: first, the texts are impeccable; second, several critical essays from which I quote appear as afterwords in those editions; third, each edition has an extremely helpful "Selected Bibliography." I recommend the Modern Library edition of *The Bostonians* (1956) and the Penguin Classic *What Maisie Knew* (1985); for all the rest, the reader can rely confidently on the Nortons: *The Scarlet Letter, Nathaniel Hawthorne's Tales, The Blithedale Romance, Tales of Henry James, The Portrait of a Lady* (2d. ed.), *The Ambassadors, The Turn of the Screw* (2d. ed.), and *Emerson's Poetry and Prose.* I have also made rather free use of the *Henry James Review,* especially the issue devoted to *Portrait* (Winter–Spring, 1986).

Other works—some old, some new, some brilliant, some awful, all interesting if only by negative example—are briefly noted here in the order in which they are cited in my book.

Stephen Donadio, "Emerson, Christian Identity, and the Dissolution of the Social Order," in *Art, Politics, and Will: Essays in Honor of Lionel Trilling* (1997) and *Nietzsche, Henry James, And the Artistic Will* (1978).
Lionel Trilling, "Our Hawthorne," in *Hawthorne Centenary Essays* (1964).
Millicent Bell, *Meaning in Henry James* (1991).
James R. Mellow, *Nathaniel Hawthorne in His Times* (1980).

Michael J. Colacurcio, "The Woman's Own Choice," in *New Essays on "The Scarlet Letter"* (1985).

Sacvan Bercovitch, "Hawthorne's A-Morality of Compromise," in the St. Martin's Press ed. of *The Scarlet Letter* (1991).

David Van Leer, "Hester's Labyrinth," in *New Essays* (1985).

Darrel Abel, *American Literature,* especially volumes 2 and 3 (1963).

David B. Davis, *Homicide and American Fiction* (1957).

Irving Howe, *Politics and the Novel* (1957) and *The American Newness* (1978).

Judith Fetterley, *The Resisting Reader: A Feminist Approach to American Fiction* (1978).

J. Hillis Miller, *Hawthorne and History* (1991).

Caroline Gordon and Allen Tate on "Young Goodman Brown" in *The House of Fiction* (1954).

Philip Horne, *Henry James and Revision* (1990).

Eve Kosofsky Sedgwick, "The Beast in the Closet: James and the Writing of Homosexual Panic," in *Sex, Politics, and Science in the Nineteenth-Century Novel,* (1986).

Shoshana Felman, "The grasp with which I recovered him," in *Henry James, The Turn of the Screw: Studies in Contemporary Criticism* (1995).

Stanley Renner, "Red hair, very red, close-curling," in ibid.

Joseph Wiesenfarth, "A Woman in *Portrait of a Lady,*" *HJR,* special *Portrait* issue (1986).

Cheryl B. Torsney, "The Political Context," ibid.

Tony Tanner, "The Fearful Self," in *Henry James: Modern Judgments* (1968).

Dorothea Krook, *The Ordeal of Consciousness in Henry James* (1962).

Peter Buitenhuis, "Introduction," *Twentieth-Century Interpretations of "The Portrait of a Lady"* (1968).

Fred Kaplan, *Henry James: The Imagination of a Genius* (1992).

Alfred Habegger, *Henry James and the "Woman Business"* (1989).

Index